Language in the Making
3

Liz Bell ● **Angela Hartley** ● **Dick Kempson**

Jane O'Donoghue ● **Nicola Telling**

Acknowledgements

Text

Pages 16–31: Extract from *Odette Churchill* by Catherine Sanders (Hamish Hamilton, 1989). Text copyright © Catherine Sanders, 1989.

Pages 32–38: Copyright © 1995 Teeny Weeny Games Ltd. *Discworld* is a Trademark Registered in the full name of Terry Pratchett.

Page 40: 'Grown up?' by John Cunliffe. *A Fifth Book of Poetry* (OUP). Reproduced by permission of David Higham Associates.

Page 44: 'At home' by John Hegley from *Can I come Down Now Dad?* Reproduced by permission of Methuen.

Page 45: 'I heard them say I'm ugly' by Elizabeth Jennings. *Collected Poems*, Carcanet. Reproduced by permission of DHA.

Page 49: 'I Am Not That Woman' by Kishwar Naheed, translated by Mahmood Jamal. Reproduced by permission of Mahmood Jamal.

Pages 58–59: 'Ode' by Gillian Allnutt. Reproduced by permission of the author.

Page 68: 'The New, Fast, Automatic Daffodils' by Adrian Henri. Copyright © 1986 Adrian Henri. Reproduced by permission of the author c/o Rogers, Coleridge and White Ltd., 20 Powis Mews, London W11 1JN.

Page 70: 'Valentine' is taken from *Mean Time* by Carol Ann Duffy published by Anvil Press Poetry in 1993.

Page 74: 'Every Breath You Take' Words by Sting © 1983, GM Sumner, UK. Reproduced by permission of EMI Music Publishing Ltd/Magnetic Publishing Ltd, London WC2H OEA.

Page 91: *The Ancient Mariner*, a play by Michael Bogdanov. Reproduced with permission of Curtis Brown Ltd, London, on behalf of Michael Bogdanov. Copyright Michael Bogdanov.

Page 96: Excerpt from Anthony Burgess's translation of *Cyrano de Bergerac* reprinted by permission of Nick Hern Books, copyright © 1985 by the Estate of Anthony Burgess.

Pages 100–101: *Don't Look Now* the screenplay adapted from the publication by Daphne du Maurier. Reproduced by permission of Rafford Films Ltd.

Pages 104–108: *Much Ado About Nothing* a screenplay by Kenneth Brannagh. Reproduced by permission of Methuen.

Pages 109–110: *Sense and Sensibility*.

Page 114: Lord Nelson's letter. An original copy of this letter is held at the British Library.

Photographs

Pages 16, 31, 74 (Paul McFagan), 85 & 87: Popperfoto.

Page 19: Permission of *The Trustees of the Imperial War Museum, London*.

Page 24: Jill MacTier.

Pages 26, 100 & 102: Canal + Image UK Limited. (Provided still from film *Odette* and gave usage permission for *Don't Look Now* still.)

Pages 32–38: Copyright © 1995 Teeny Weeny Games Ltd.

Pages 49–50: © Peter Sanders Photography.

Pages 58, 70 & 72: Alison MacTier

Page 77: Clipboard: Kelvin Freeman.

Page 83: Russell Stinton.

Page 97: *Cyrano de Bergerac*, permission to use still from film granted by SYGMA.

Page 103: *Kiss of Death* 20th Century Fox (Courtesy Kobal).

Pages 105 & 107: *Much Ado About Nothing*, permission to use still from film granted by Renaissance Films.

Page 109: *Sense and Sensibility*. Courtesy of Columbia Pictures/Tristar/Columbia Tristar International Television. Copyright © 1999 Columbia Pictures Industries Inc. All Rights reserved. (Courtesy Kobal).

Page 113: Lord Nelson by Sir William Beechey (1753–1839) Cider House Galleries Ltd., Bletchingley/Bridgeman Art Library, London/New York.

Illustrations

Rebecca Allen (Big Time Pictures): Pages 40–41, 48.

Tony O'Donnell: Page 99.

Gillian Hunt (Specs Art): Pages 6–15, 44–47, 80–83, 89.

Brian Lee (Graham–Cameron Illustration): Pages 21–23, 25, 28, 52, 61, 64–65 (parchment), 90–94, 101–102, 116.

Every effort has been made to contact copyright holders of material used in this book. If any have been overlooked, we will be pleased to make any necessary arrangements.

Editor: Alison MacTier Design: Turners Creative, Dunstable; Crow Trees Design Layout Artist: Tracey Baker – Flare Repro, Hertford Cover Design: Ed Gallagher

© 1999 Folens Limited, on behalf of the authors.

First published 1999 by Folens Limited, Dunstable and Dublin.

Folens Limited, Albert House, Apex Business Centre, Boscombe Road, Dunstable, LU5 4RL, England.

ISBN 1 86202725 0
Printed in Singapore by Craft Print

Contents

Prose

Poetry

Script & Speech

Introduction

Language in the Making is a rich and rewarding series intended for classroom use. With its varied texts and activities, the series aims to involve, challenge and stimulate pupils. Above all, it aims to encourage pupils to shape and form their writing deliberately – making conscious language decisions in real language settings – so that they are **making and crafting language**.

This textbook is divided into three main parts:
- Prose
- Poetry
- Script & Speech

These parts are followed by photocopiable assessment tests and a glossary.

This book contains a number of extracts from both familiar texts and texts that some pupils may not recognise. These range from Sojourner Truth's speech 'Ain't I a Woman?', Coleridge's *The Rime of the Ancient Mariner* and Shakespeare's *Macbeth*, through to *Cyrano de Bergerac* and the real-life story of wartime spy Odette Churchill.

The activities encourage pupils to shape and mould language to suit given situations or roles, whether it is as a writer of a fantasy narrative for computer games such as *Discworld*, a screenwriter composing a treatment for presentation to a film production company, or a lyricist for a pop group. The students are asked to make decisions about the appropriate grammar, punctuation, tone, layout, or other conventions, for each given situation.

Each part has three sections:
- **section one** provides a **personal focus** in which feelings and ideas are communicated strongly from a personal perspective, for example in letter form between friends (page 6).
- **section two develops notions of form** in which students adapt, revise and extend texts having looked at common conventions, for example how odes have been used by modern writers (page 58).
- **section three** takes a commercial or professional approach to language, asking students to take on a specific role, such as a screenwriter presenting his or her ideas at a production meeting (page 112).

The units within those sections are aided by a series of clear headings.
- **Focus** outlines what is expected of students within the unit.
- **Starting** introduces the forthcoming text(s) and activities.
- **Preparing** and **Planning** are progressive stages leading to **Presenting** (in which a major assignment or task is completed).
- **Follow-up** offers further activities and extensions.
- **Language Decisions** asks students to reflect on sentence grammar, layout and conventions.
- **Language Pointers** give useful, clear guidance and definitions, either as new information or as revision of previous knowledge.

Grammatical points or language features are highlighted, both in the text, and in the Language Pointers box in the top right corner. The Glossary functions as a revision of these terms and a cross reference to pages on which they appear.

Prose

FOCUS FOCUS

UNIT 1

● *Examine the use of verbs, adjectives and adverbs.*
● *Write an account of an unsuccessful holiday.*

A word between friends

STARTING

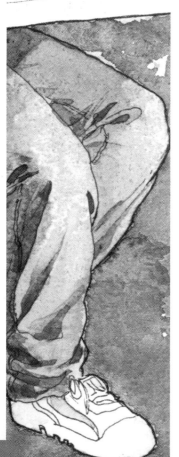

1. Carla and Ben were brought up in the same street. Over the years, from the age of seven, they have been friends. They have kept every card and letter they have sent to each other. Now, both aged twenty-three, they are looking back through some of the things they have written.

When Carla was thirteen she wrote this note:

> Dear Ben,
>
> This is just a quick note to say we've arrived safely. The flight was endless and it was very late when we got to the hotel. The man on reception seemed confused and everyone got really annoyed.
>
> This morning is sunny and hot. I feel so white compared to everyone else who is tanned and good-looking. I feel too sleepy to write so I'll stop now.
>
> Luv,
> Carla

Almost ten years later, Carla went on a very similar holiday. When she wrote a letter to Ben on this occasion, she found herself using a whole variety of words to get her message across:

> Dear Ben,
>
> Together with the other undead of Flight B111, we transferred to the Hotel Bel Mar in the early hours of the morning. Corralled into the foyer, we manoeuvred suitcases like the backsides of cattle and mooed faintly with irritation until we had been organised.
>
> Thus it was late this morning when I stepped across the baking stones surrounding the pool. Every other body is sleek as well as brown. In contrast, should I have fallen on those stones, I'd have dropped like wet dough.
>
> Now settled in a lounger, I find I can barely write this. My eyes cannot accommodate the severe contrasts of sun and shade. Every drop of water reflects prisms of light. My attention dissolves inside these baubles and I want to do nothing but sleep here for the week, half connected to everything and nothing.
>
> Yours,
> Carla

6

- An **adjective** describes a **noun**, and is often found in front of it – 'the *quick, brown* fox'. It is also used with the **verb** 'to be' – 'he is *foolish* and *unreliable*'.
- An **adverb** modifies a sentence, and explains how a **verb** works – 'she slid *dangerously*'. It can modify an **adjective** or another **adverb** – 'it was *so* ugly' or 'he played *really badly*'.
- A **verb** describes an action or a state – 'she *hurried* down the hall', 'she *wondered* who it *could* be'.

PREPARING

2. In Carla's earlier note, almost all the 'energy' words are **adjectives**. There are eleven of them. With a partner, find and list them.

3. Now make a note of any differences you notice between the note and the letter Carla wrote when she was older. Look particularly at her use of **verbs**.

The same year that Carla went to Spain, Ben went on a narrow-boat holiday during the early part of the summer term. This was his postcard:

Dear Carla,

If the rain hasn't washed this message off, I've not drowned yet. It's been raining continually. Tim argues mindlessly over every little thing and Dad loses his temper occasionally over nothing at all. There's nothing to do and I'm missing you and everyone else. Write back quickly to me and tell me how well you're all doing. I need cheering up badly.

Ben

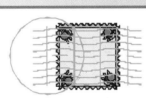

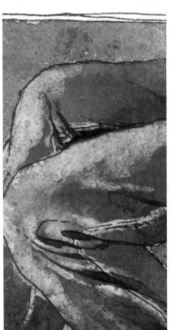

4. Many of Ben's energy words are **adverbs**. With a partner, find and list six of them.

5. Write an account of Ben's wet holiday on the narrow boat using more varied language. Take the contents of the postcard and describe those things in more detail. Use Carla's letter at the bottom of page 6 as a model.

PRESENTING

FOCUS FOCUS

UNIT 2

● *Examine and make use of conceits.*

Conceits

STARTING

1. Ben used his letters as a way of entertaining Carla. This is a key feature of personal letters, and Ben did this by developing **conceits** – short fantasies created from the ordinary, everyday things around him. Below are two examples from the letters he sent to Carla.

The first is from one summer when Carla and everybody else, except for Ben, seem to have gone on holiday. Once again, she is in Spain:

Dear Carla,

I'm sure you've barely had time to read this as you stagger from one Carnival to the next Fiesta to a Sierra and even to the Galaxy beyond, but since I can't afFORD a fancy holiday, I'm stuck here alone.

Mum and Dad are so guilty for failing to provide even the basic subsistence-level foreign holiday that they have abandoned their earthly bodies which now stand vaguely in doorways, loiter in shops, or tread the lawn, smiling wanly.

I could walk out of our house right now in the certain knowledge that I would neither see nor hear anyone. Strewn across driveways and at junctions I would no doubt find the occasional flip-flop or sun-block aftershave. I could scream blue murder and no one would express any interest in the deaths, let alone the colour of them.

Tell me you're having a terrible time in Spain.

Ben

8

▶ **Language Pointer** ◀

● **Conceits** are often clever fantasies or language tricks linked to one idea, conjured up to amuse and entertain an **audience**. Strictly speaking, they are not true, but they use **exaggeration** to make an amusing point.

Ben also wrote to Carla when he went away on a school Geography field trip when he was 15. Carla wasn't there. She'd taken History; in fact, Ben has no idea why he'd chosen Geography in the first place.

Dear Carla,

For the first time in my life, I see the point of maps; they exist so you don't have to go anywhere. All you have to do to see the geography is – turn the page. Unfortunately, we've got to walk another five miles up a hill so Nixon can stop us all in our tracks with the stunning observation that 'here is hill' and 'there is not hill or valley' and that 'valleys occur where hills are not' and vice versa. At which point we'll all draw pictures.

The school should have made us take a medical last year before we were allowed to opt for Geography. It seems that Geography requires you to enjoy walking all over the countryside before retiring to sleep in something resembling a stable where quite possibly in an adjoining stable a girl in your form is about to give birth to the baby Jesus, as there's no room at the Inn – except for eight boys from the year above and that young PE teacher …

I could go on and on … like this field trip – but I won't.

Back soon,
            Ben

2. Each of the **paragraphs** in the two letters contains a different **conceit**. Write down a brief explanation of each one. For example, the first one makes a clever link between Spain and a certain popular make of car.

PREPARING

3. Ben has been on other trips too. On one occasion he went to London for an overnight stay, followed by some Christmas shopping with his parents, which he was supposed to enjoy.

PRESENTING

Write about one of the following:

● This episode from Ben's point of view as a comic fantasy which gives a clear indication of the experience.
● An experience of your own which you turn into a series of comic **conceits** to entertain the reader.

FOCUS FOCUS

UNIT 3

● Encounter and practise the use of satire in personal letters.
● Examine and make use of exaggeration in a variety of written forms.

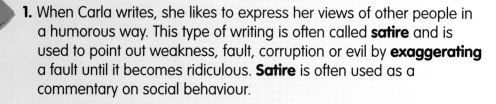

Comical commentaries

STARTING

1. When Carla writes, she likes to express her views of other people in a humorous way. This type of writing is often called **satire** and is used to point out weakness, fault, corruption or evil by **exaggerating** a fault until it becomes ridiculous. **Satire** is often used as a commentary on social behaviour.

Carla uses a light form of **satire** in her writing. Here are two examples in her letters.

Firstly she writes about her father:

You know how my father is when you meet him and how he's quite impressive? Well, when you stay with him he becomes the most revolting slob imaginable. He has this thing of scratching himself, you know, all over. And he's not comfortable in his armchair until he's practically lying flat out in the most uncomfortable position with no support from his backside out. And he watches TV even when he tells you it's rubbish and gradually he creates his own refuse zone of cups, papers, plates, mags, letters, peels, wrappers and all sorts. And when he gets up, he leaves it all behind, except you can see this shape in the middle that was his body, like when they draw a chalk outline round a dead body in American cop shows ...

In this next letter she writes about a tutor at college:

I hate my new tutor. I couldn't exactly say he's done anything I could exactly write to the Pope about or pass off as criminally insane but that's half the problem. He is the most patronising, superior, oily drip I've ever had the misfortune to deal with. He tells me my work is rubbish, in so many words, then smiles. Is he pleased? Should I celebrate? And when I ask him questions he smiles and nods his head. "Ah, yes," he says, as if that was the crux of the whole issue, and then nothing, just smiles. I suspect he hasn't a clue what he's talking about and has got away with seeming clever for years by avoiding saying anything at all of any use or relevance to anyone. "What's the meaning of life?" "Hmm, pertinent." And everyone thinks he knows the answer. Well, I'm going to find some way of putting a bomb under his chair and blowing him out of the window. Clear the atmosphere, getting rid of some of that 'smug' ...

2. Look back at the two extracts and note down the parts you think are **exaggerated**. Perhaps neither of them is!

PREPARING

3. With your partner, list three characters from TV you are familiar with. If you were to make fun of them add, firstly, what it is you would make fun of and, secondly, whether you could describe it with **exaggeration** for comic effect. The example below is a made-up character.

PLANNING

Name	Feature	Exaggeration
Davey Flashman (game-show host)	loud, repetitive comments, terrible songs	when he sings, nightingales fall off their branches with embarrassment

4. Choose some people you know or have come across. Decide what it is about them you wish to **exaggerate** and write a **satirical** piece about them.

PRESENTING

You may do it:

- in the form of a letter to a friend

- in the form of a feature in a paper (if it is about someone well known)

- in the form of a **narrative** story.

● *Consider how personal letters both reveal and withhold the truth.*
● *Examine and experiment with different styles of letter writing.*

The truth and not the whole truth

STARTING

1. Sometimes it is easy to write honestly in a letter to a close friend but equally the relationship can sometimes make it difficult.

I wish it hadn't happened

Everything's fine Mum

PREPARING

2. Think of a crisis that might happen to you. Decide to whom you could speak about it and how much you could tell them. Express this as a percentage: if you could tell them half the story, it would be 50%. Give each of your parents, relatives and friends a number, or write their names if you prefer, and set out in a table how much of the **truth** you think you could tell them, as in the example below:

Friend or relative	Percentage of the truth
1	90%
2	60%
3	10%
4	40%
5	5%
6	0%

Carla has been through a similar situation. On a Sunday afternoon in early November a few years ago, Carla wrote letters to her parents and to Ben. She also wrote a piece in her diary. She was in her first term away from home at college.

Read what she wrote on the next page.

- **Truth** and **fiction** are not necessarily opposite ideas. If you don't tell your reader absolutely everything, you can mislead them, even if you don't actually tell any lies.

  Similarly, there can be different versions of the truth; what seemed to have happened in one person's eyes may not have occurred in another's.

I've been really proud of the way I've managed the money so far, but I can see I'm going to spend a lot towards the end of term and then there's Christmas. I've got to do something over the holidays to earn money, so if you hear of anything, let me know.

I've been much happier too. I think there's a real crowd of us now, people I get on with and can trust. They drop in on me and that still gives me a buzz, entertaining in my own place! Work's fine and the weekend's been a busy one – lots of us helping someone move flat. We had a bit of a party after all that work, to celebrate.

This is an extract from Carla's letter to her parents.

Last night was the best party since I've been here with everyone just so happy and part of a group. There were really fast, mad times and times when you'd be talking with someone and then not see them again but not worry because you each had equally good mates to be with. Everyone just mixed and there were no tensions. We were in Sanji's new place. It was still a complete mess but it was all there. I've been sleeping most of today but I've just got up to eat and write this to you.

This is from her letter to Ben.

Below is the entry in her diary.

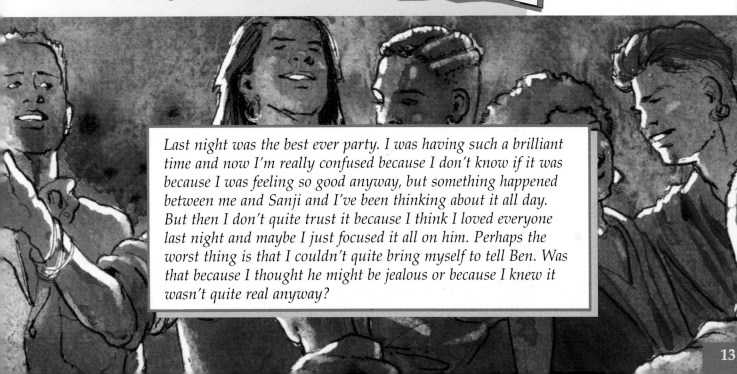

Last night was the best ever party. I was having such a brilliant time and now I'm really confused because I don't know if it was because I was feeling so good anyway, but something happened between me and Sanji and I've been thinking about it all day. But then I don't quite trust it because I think I loved everyone last night and maybe I just focused it all on him. Perhaps the worst thing is that I couldn't quite bring myself to tell Ben. Was that because I thought he might be jealous or because I knew it wasn't quite real anyway?

13

The truth and not the whole truth

3. Late in the afternoon, when she had been going over things without resolving anything in her own mind, Carla felt she had to communicate with Sanji. She decided a letter was the right way to do it. After several attempts, she had one she could take round and put through his letter box. Read the letter below:

Look, when you pick this up off the floor, you're going to think it's really silly because, obviously, I will have just been to your door in order to push it under and, surely, it would be much more sensible to come in and talk to you. But sometimes, somehow, a letter is just better because I can say what I want to say and not be embarrassed about you being there to listen.

But then, at the same time, it's easy to get the tone wrong when reading a letter. So this is not heavy and deep, just easy and casual, and all about trying to figure out exactly where we are, because we're going to bump into each other tomorrow and I couldn't stand it if it was awkward and we didn't know what to say or we didn't say anything at all and we misunderstood each other, or whatever.

So, this is what I need to say to you before I meet you again but don't want to say when I meet you.

I had a wonderful time last night; I don't know when I was last so happy. And being with you was part of that and that makes you very special to me. But, but, but, that doesn't mean I'm expecting anything to come of it, or not to come of it, so don't feel any strain when you meet me tomorrow. Let it be like it always is and if, some other time when we've got time, we want to talk then so be it. But tomorrow, don't lose our closeness and our easiness.

Thanks for yesterday. Looking forward to seeing you soon.

Your very good friend,

Carla

4. Copy and complete this table, showing the issues and feelings that Carla deals with in the content of the four pieces on page 13 and 14. Consider also any changes of **style**, length of time spent on particular subjects, and what Carla is using language for: to tell, request, wonder about something or explain.

	Parents' letter	Ben's letter	Diary	Sanji's letter
Issues	money, holiday work, friends, her own place, the party			whether to write or speak to Sanji; problems with seeing Sanji the next day
feelings		range of emotions at the party: happiness; feelings of being part of a group; feeling tired		
style				questioning, uncertain, reflecting, exploring, speculating, feelings expressed in the first person the next day

5. Think of an episode that might happen to you. Write to someone you can tell some of it to, then to someone you can tell more of it to, and create an entry for your diary where the most important things can be considered.

PRESENTING

6. You know a little about Carla and Ben now. Imagine Ben found out about Carla's 'fling', if that's what it was, with Sanji. Write a sequence of letters between them and try to maintain some of the characteristics of their writing, for example: Ben's enjoyment of words and playing with ideas; Carla's tendency to be cutting, if she chooses.

FOLLOW-UP

- Divide a story into parts.
- Convert notes into continuous prose.
- Look at how paragraphs are used.

UNIT 1

SPY

1. The work in this unit focuses on **autobiography** and **biography** – both forms of prose writing that feature elements of **narrative fiction** and information texts. As you will see, **biographies** tell the stories of peoples' lives. On the following pages you are going to be the **biographer**, and you will tell the story of the life of Odette Churchill (pictured below) and the part she played in the Second World War.

Why Odette Churchill?

This photo, taken in February 1947, tells us little about Odette. Using her own words, she might be viewed as just an 'ordinary woman'. But, as you will see, Odette Churchill was anything but ordinary; she had a fascinating, often dangerous, life and played a part in one of the greatest conflicts the world has seen. What's more, the story of her life doesn't only tell us about her life, but also about historical events and the lives of people she came into contact with.

2. What do biographies and autobiographies do?

Think back over last weekend. If you were to tell the story of that weekend, decide which five things you would write about. Note down a title for each of the five topics and choose an order. What you are left with is similar to the structure for an **autobiography** – five selected moments or events that are connected to you to a greater or lesser degree.

So, who was Odette Churchill – and what was her story?

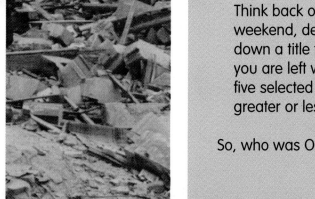

3. The following notes have been made for an opening chapter on the wartime experiences of Odette Churchill. They create the background to her story. Read carefully through the two sets of notes below.

- 1 September 1939 – Germany invades Poland.
- 3 September 1939 – France and Britain at war with Germany.
- September 1939 – children evacuated from British cities.
- April 1940 – Germany invades Denmark and Norway, takes Holland in four days, Belgium in three weeks and France in seven weeks – known as a 'lightning war' or '*Blitzkrieg*'.
- May 1940 – British retreat from Europe through Dunkirk.
- Summer 1940 – battle between British and German air forces, known as 'the Battle of Britain'.
- 7 September 1940 – bombing of London begins, known as 'the Blitz'.
- November 1940 – over 10 000 killed in the Blitz.

- Britain must get back into Europe to win war.
- Early 1940 – Special Operations Executive (SOE) set up to send recruits 'behind the lines' to help resistance groups fight Nazis using guerrilla tactics.
- SOE seeks volunteers who know France and speak French.
- Spring 1942 – War Office advertises for photos of the European coastline, seeking French speakers.

4. Now write down a title for each set of notes. Think carefully – 'War' is too general, and could apply to both.

SPY

5. Now read these two further sets of notes and give each of them a title which sums up their content.

Odette:
- sends photos of herself and brother playing on the beach at Boulogne
- is called to the War Office
- when asked to volunteer, replies that she is just an ordinary woman, housewife and mother and doesn't believe she is suitable
- thinks about what might have happened to her own three children had she still been in France, and about her mother still living there
- leaves her children at boarding school with an aunt to look after them in the holidays
- tells everyone she is being posted to Scotland
- leaves for training in a country house where she is called Céline and speaks only French.

Before the First World War, women used to obtain information from men using their physical attractiveness. By the Second World War, where there was work that both men and women could do, women were selected for it on the same terms as men.

Odette is taught, among other things:
- to operate a wireless transmitter
- shooting
- Morse code
- map reading
- self-defence
- poaching
- avoiding capture
- responding to arrest
- working in teams and with local resistance groups.

▶ Language Pointers ◀

- A **paragraph** begins on a new line and is either **indented** (set in from the margin) or **blocked** (arranged with a whole line space between each **paragraph**).
- Each **paragraph** is a section of writing which usually contains a new topic, or a change of time or place.

PRESENTING

6. Now turn the four sets of notes (including the two from page 17) into four **paragraphs**. Set out each **paragraph** clearly by either **indenting** or **blocking**. You may leave out parts of the information given or add points and observations of your own. Write in full sentences. For example:

Odette is taught to operate a wireless

Odette was given the following report at the end of her assessment:

> "Céline has enthusiasm and seems to have absorbed the teaching ... . She is, however, impulsive and hasty in her judgements ... . She is excitable and temperamental although she has a certain determination ... . Her main asset is her patriotism ... . Her main weakness is her complete unwillingness to admit she could ever be wrong."

With this report she should probably have been rejected. One of the SOE section heads appointed her on instinct.

FOLLOW-UP

7. With a partner, discuss whether she is a suitable person to work in secret in France. One of you should argue for her and one against, using the report and any other information that you've read as evidence for your arguments.

- Anticipate the detail involved in preparing an agent for life in another country.
- Check the terms biography and autobiography.
- Convert narrative text from first to third person.

DANGER

1. Before you read about Odette's experiences, imagine you are preparing someone to go into occupied France. With a partner, discuss what you must do to make sure they will fit into French life without being detected.

Odette was, indeed, sent to France where she became a successful agent. Women were often asked to do the most dangerous work as they were more likely to be able to move about undetected.

Final preparations

Odette was first briefed in great detail about day-to-day life in France, including the use of ration cards and the latest fashions. Her clothes were given French labels and her teeth French fillings, her wedding ring filed off and replaced. She wrote a huge pile of letters to her children that the SOE would post at intervals. She was given a poison pill which would kill her in six seconds if she needed it. She memorised her instructions:

Code name: LISE.   **Destination:** Auxerre.

- To be received by RAOUL in Cannes.
- To cross demarcation line to Auxerre.
- To get established and obtain details of WT [wireless transmitter] operator in Paris for communicating with London.

Mission: To find a 'safe' house for agents and escapers. To recruit local members to the circuit and supply information.

Password: *"Connaissez-vous un bon coiffeur par ici?"* (Do you know of a good hairdresser round here?)

Reply: *"Cela dépend de ce que vous voulez dire par bon."* (That all depends what you mean by good.)

Language Pointers

- **Autobiography** comes from Greek and means, literally, 'self, life, write'. It is an account of your own life.
- A **biography** is an account of someone's life written by another person.
- **Narrative** is a more general term, relating to any linked chain of events told by someone – usually a story.

Getting to France

The plan was for Odette to fly to Gibraltar and take a boat to Cannes on the French coast. On her first attempt, another plane crashed into hers prior to take-off. On the second attempt, the Gestapo – the German secret police – arrested the French due to receive her. Next, bad weather intervened. Then, her plane crashed on take-off and finished up on the edge of a cliff.

Finally, she took a troopship. The Polish captain pointed to a great pile of washing-up and ordered Odette to do it because she was a woman. She had to, with cold sea water. The captain was often drunk. She threw his whisky supply over the side and when he found out, he nearly strangled her. She was lucky to get to France at all.

A first assignment

Odette's first assignment was to travel from Cannes to Marseilles with two other agents to deliver 200 000 francs hidden in a newspaper to an agent in a café and collect a suitcase with plans of the docks at Marseilles.

It all went well until she missed her last train back. She was left having to take a bed in a brothel used by the Germans. When the German military police raided the brothel looking for deserters, the manageress saved Odette by claiming she was her niece and was suffering from highly contagious scarlet fever.

DANGER

Although she settled into life as an agent in France, things were never easy.

A lucky escape

Life as an agent involved long periods of boredom punctuated by short periods of excitement and danger. On one occasion, her group was ambushed at night waiting for a plane to do a pick up. Odette ran off, chased by a tracker dog. To make the dog lose her scent, she plunged into an icy river, waited until the curfew was over and walked ten kilometres into town.

'I decided to brazen it out by sitting in full view on a café terrace hoping the others would find me. At the next table four Germans were saying how easy it would be to catch the fugitives!'

▶ **Language Pointers** ◀

- A **biography** is usually written in the third person. The third person singular uses the **subject pronouns** *he, she* and *it* before the **verb**. The third person plural uses the **subject pronoun** *they*. The **object pronouns** include *him* and *her* and *them*. The **possessive pronouns** include *his, hers* and *theirs*.
- An **autobiography** is usually written in the first person. The first person singular **subject pronoun** is *I*. The first person plural **subject pronoun** is *we*. The **object pronouns** are *me* and *us*. The **possessive pronouns** are *mine* and *ours*.
- There are other changes between first and third person **narratives**. For instance, the **verb** may need to change to maintain agreement. If the first person *I run* is to be changed to the third person, the **verb** would have to change too – *he runs*.

*... chased by
a tracker dog.*

PRESENTING

2. On your own, read through the account of Odette's life in France given in the sections entitled 'Getting to France', 'A first assignment' (page 21) and 'A lucky escape' (page 22). Convert this third person **narrative** to a first person **narrative** as if it was an **autobiography** and this was Odette's own account of her life.

It would begin: '*The plan was for me to fly to Gibraltar ...*'.

3. When everyone has prepared the whole text, take it in turns to read out a paragraph at a time to the class in the first person.

FOLLOW-UP

4. Take one of the moments identified in 'A lucky escape' and write a full description of what happened, including your (Odette's) feelings, what you saw, and exactly what happened.

*I plunged
into an icy river ...*

- Plan a response to an agent's dilemma.
- Understand the differences between spoken and standard English.
- Convert a transcript of speech into standard English.

BETRAYAL

STARTING

1. When Odette arrived in France, she teamed up with an Englishman, Peter Churchill (code named Raoul) and their wireless operator, Arnaud. The following is an imaginary recording of the event by Peter Churchill, based on fact, from February 1943, St Jorioz, near Lake Annecy.

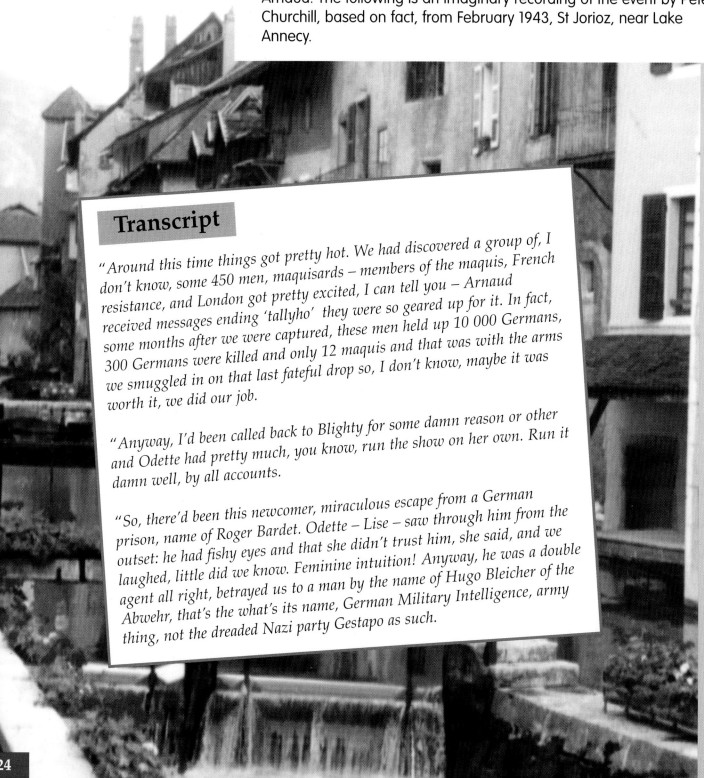

Transcript

" Around this time things got pretty hot. We had discovered a group of, I don't know, some 450 men, maquisards — members of the maquis, French resistance, and London got pretty excited, I can tell you — Arnaud received messages ending 'tallyho' they were so geared up for it. In fact, some months after we were captured, these men held up 10 000 Germans, 300 Germans were killed and only 12 maquis and that was with the arms we smuggled in on that last fateful drop so, I don't know, maybe it was worth it, we did our job.

"Anyway, I'd been called back to Blighty for some damn reason or other and Odette had pretty much, you know, run the show on her own. Run it damn well, by all accounts.

"So, there'd been this newcomer, miraculous escape from a German prison, name of Roger Bardet. Odette — Lise — saw through him from the outset: he had fishy eyes and that she didn't trust him, she said, and we laughed, little did we know. Feminine intuition! Anyway, he was a double agent all right, betrayed us to a man by the name of Hugo Bleicher of the Abwehr, that's the what's its name, German Military Intelligence, army thing, not the dreaded Nazi party Gestapo as such.

▶ **Language Pointers** ◀

● A **transcript** is a record of speech, written exactly as it is spoken, word for word.
● **Standard English** is the accepted form of English as it would be written in business correspondence and other formal texts.

PREPARING

2. You are working as an agent like Odette. A German comes to you to tell you that he has vital information which can bring about an end to the war. He asks you to arrange to send him to England. You don't believe him but you must be careful since he clearly knows who you are. Note down your plan of action and then explain it to a partner.

The account continues:

> "So, what happened, Bardet got Odette's name to Bleicher, he visited her, asked to be taken to England, said he had plans to bring an end to the war. Of course, Odette didn't believe him, told him he'd have to wait for the next full moon to go, date would be … um … April 18th, yes I think the 18th. So, she got everyone else the hell out of there. I parachuted in on the 15th with all the equipment and arms right up in the mountains, in the dark, in the snow, 2000 metres up there on the mountainside, just Arnaud, Odette and Jean Cottet, the hotel manager from where we were staying.
>
> "Little did we know there was also another double agent at work at the London HQ. Anyway, middle of the next night, knock on the door. Odette goes down. There's Bleicher staring coolly at her and there are three guns trained on her. She's hustled upstairs, I'm shaken awake, handcuffed. I didn't know at the time but Odette had spotted my wallet which contained vital new radio codes and names. Somehow, God knows how she managed it, but somehow, she hid it in her clothes and pushed it down the car seat as we were driven away.
>
> "I couldn't handle the imprisonment, I don't mind telling you, tried to escape, got beaten up. Apparently, Odette claimed we were married, I was a member of the Churchill family and that I'd nothing really to do with the work we were engaged in. Sadly for her, they tended to believe her. Anyway we were handed over to the Gestapo at Toulon, then to Paris and the notorious Fresnes prison."

PLANNING

3. In pairs, study the **transcript** and list the features you think would not be acceptable in a version written in **standard English**. Share these as a class. These features might include abbreviations, slang and so on.

PRESENTING

4. Write a version of Peter's account in the third person, in **standard English**.

It might begin: 'At the time of the move, the pace of events quickened. They had discovered …'

- *Plan strategies for surviving solitary confinement.*
- *Send information in its most reduced form.*
- *Decide which parts of speech carry this basic information.*

TORTURE

STARTING

1. You are held in solitary confinement. You do not know how long for. The room is only three metres by four metres and contains only a bed and a high window. Share your strategies for survival with a partner.

IMPRISONMENT

When she arrived at Fresnes prison, Odette was roughly strip-searched by a grim wardress and marched to cell No. 108. It contained a rusty bed, a broken chair, a tin bowl and spoon, a lavatory, a cold water tap and a basin and was only three metres by four metres. It was 8 May 1943, and she would spend the next seven months in solitary confinement here.

In solitary confinement twenty-four hours are endless — sometimes I felt there was no difference between twenty-four hours and twenty-four months. The only way to escape is with your mind. After all, no one can control our minds if we don't want them to.

Odette

She learned to tap on the walls to communicate with other prisoners. She kept a record of the days and months scratched on the dirty wall with a hairgrip. She shut out the screams and shouts of the prison and escaped into her mind: stories and songs from childhood; redecorating the rooms in all the houses she knew; imagining her children and talking to them. Every day she turned her skirt round an inch to prevent it wearing out.

> ## Language Pointers

● **Simple language** in certain circumstances can convey meaning without key parts of a clause, such as a **verb**. For example, if Odette sent a message saying '*In danger*', then the meaning would be reasonably clear.

On thirteen occasions, Odette was taken to Gestapo headquarters where she suffered severe torture.

The SOE had told me what to expect. But the Gestapo made a great mistake — they put me in a chair facing the window. I could see the sky and the trees of the Bois de Boulogne. I thought, if I keep focusing on that, I can get away from all this, because I hadn't seen trees for so long.

If you look into the eyes of the man who is torturing you he knows he cannot win. You are stronger than he is. He can kill you but that is all. ... You have to fight each day's battle as it comes. You have to recognise that you may lose the last battle.

Odette

Luckily for Odette, a senior officer came in and observed that she would never talk and they let her go. Several days later, in the Gestapo court, she was condemned to death without trial on two counts, as a French woman and as a British spy. She remarked that she could only die once.

A red cross, meaning condemned, was painted across her door. In the end, months passed and, finally, she caught pneumonia. The prison captain and the chaplain rescued her and put her in a warmer cell with three other women. She was allowed to work in the sewing room but refused to make or repair German uniforms. Instead, she made two dolls from bits of old underwear, scraps and bedding straw as Christmas presents for the chaplain's niece and nephew. After the war, thinking she would be dead, the chaplain sent them back to England to be passed on to her own children.

> **PRESENTING**

While Odette was in Fresnes prison she communicated with the other prisoners by tapping on the wall. Obviously, it would be important to reduce messages to their barest minimum.

2. Write down three messages by which Odette could tell the girl in the next cell about herself. Reduce them to the simplest, shortest expression.

3. Decide as a class which parts of speech carry information in its simplest form.

- *Read the final stage of Odette's story.*

CONDEMNED

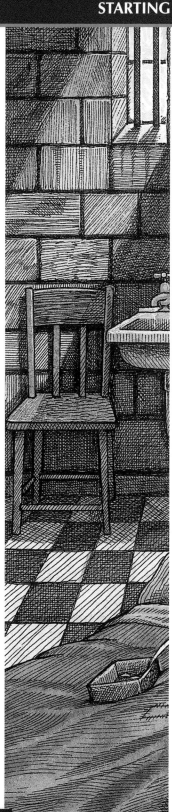

STARTING

1. Although Odette had temporarily escaped execution she was still a captive, and known to be a French spy. Her ordeals were not over yet.

In Germany

In May 1944, Odette left France for Germany, where she spent eight weeks in Karlsruhe prison. During this time, on 6 June 1944, Allied troops landed in Normandy and the Resistance began to fight openly. No doubt because of this, Odette was moved further into Germany, to Frankfurt. Here, prisoners were locked in cages in a huge room where harsh lights were kept permanently on.

Next, she travelled by cattle truck to Halle where she shared an attic with a huddled mass of women.

Finally, she arrived at Ravensbruck Concentration Camp, where the commandant, Fritz Suhren, sent her to an underground cell. Once a month, the darkness was split by light and Suhren appeared in the doorway. He would ask her if she had anything to say, to which she would answer, "No," and he would disappear again. Again she retreated into her own mind to survive the isolation and permanent darkness. One of the things she did here was to design, cut and make clothes for her children in her imagination.

In August, Allied armies landed in the area of southern France where Odette had worked. To punish her, the Nazis turned up her heating, blocked off the ventilation and starved her for a week. She became so ill, they took her to the camp hospital. They diagnosed dysentery, scurvy and tuberculosis among other things but did not treat her. On the way back from the hospital, she managed to pick up a leaf which she held in her hand as she was forced to listen to the dreadful atrocities of the final days at the camp.

Language Pointer

● **Implied meanings** – the leaf that Odette picks up has implied significance. Nothing is said here to explain why it is important, but the implication is that it is a **symbol** of growth and life, which Odette holds on to – both literally and **metaphorically**.

Because I was so ill they left my fan light open and the cinders floated on to my bed. Towards the end I could hear the screams of the women forced into the crematorium.

Odette

In mid-April 1945, orders came from Berlin that all bunker prisoners were to be executed so that there would be no surviving witnesses. Perhaps as bargaining tools, Suhren kept seven alive, including Odette. At 6am on her birthday, 28 April, Odette was taken from her cell to a luxurious Mercedes with Suhren and driven out of the camp to a village occupied by the US army. Odette asked for his gun and briefcase and told the US soldiers who Fritz Suhren was and requested that he be made their prisoner.

When I first saw daylight after months of darkness it was an extraordinary feeling. I felt I was almost literally drinking the air and swallowing it down. It was almost painful and I could not face the light at first.

That first night of my release was unforgettable. It was a glorious night, full of stars and very cold. The Americans wanted to find me a bed for the night but I preferred to sit in the car. It was so long since I had seen the night sky.

Odette

● Consider the ways a biography
  might be researched and
  prepared.
● List, discuss and write an essay
  on the impact of childhood on
  the behaviour of an adult.

CHILDHOOD

STARTING

1. It seems odd to read about Odette's childhood, at the end of her story. But, in reading about it, consider the woman she became.

Childhood

Odette was born on 28 April 1912, in Amiens, northern France. She was the eldest child of Gaston and Yvonne Brailly. When she was two, the First World War broke out and some of the fiercest fighting took place in the region where she lived. Her father, twice decorated for bravery, was killed when she was four. Her mother, left to bring up Odette and her brother on little money, moved in with her father's parents. In 1918 the war ended.

The children were then brought up by Odette's grandfather. He was a retired naval officer and a great believer in the importance of strength of character and discipline. As a test of courage, Odette, who was petrified of the dark, was often made to go into the garden at night to fetch his spectacles.

After church, on Sundays, her grandfather would take the children to their father's grave. He would tell them that there would be another war in twenty years in which they must also do their duty.

When she was seven, Odette caught polio. There was no known treatment. So she had to lie on her back for nearly a year and could hardly move. Her grandfather did all he could to strengthen her spirit. She recalled how she was never allowed to feel sorry for herself, to accept what comes and make the best of it.

Odette recovered from polio, but soon afterwards she went blind. Her grandfather and family kept her occupied with stories, songs and poems, which she stored up in her memory. She was cut off from school and friends but did not mind. Finally, her mother found a herbalist who was able to restore her sight.

PREPARING

2. Producing a **biography** involves a great deal of work before the writing itself can be done. Imagine writing in the 1950s when most of the main characters in Odette's story were still alive. Discuss with a partner in detail what you would need to do and who you would need to see.

▶ **Language Pointer** ◀

● A **biographer** needs to compile a store of facts, background information (historical or social) and also opinions or memories from those who know the subject.

3. List all the elements of her childhood which you think contributed to Odette's ability to face the challenges of her adult life.

PLANNING

4. Write a short essay explaining exactly how each of these elements played its part.

PRESENTING

This kind of psychological insight into the character and make-up of an individual is very much part of the role of the **biographer**.

Postscript

During the war, in order to save Peter Churchill, she had pretended they were husband and wife. After the war, they were married. She was later awarded an MBE and the George Cross.

Odette and Tania Szabo looking at a memorial tablet to Britain's war heroines.
The list of names included Tania's mother, Violette Szabo.

I am a very ordinary woman, to whom a chance has been given, to see human beings at their best and at their worst. I knew kindness as well as cruelty, understanding as well as brutality. I completely believe in the potential nobility of the human spirit.

Odette

FOCUS
FOCUS
UNIT 1

- *Study the mock-heroic form.*
- *Write in mock-heroic style.*

STARTING

1. In 1995 the computer games company, Psygnosis, released an adventure game created by the software developers Teeny Weeny Games, based on the world of Terry Pratchett's hugely successful novel series, *Discworld.* They were given the background and the central character, but computer games need to be carefully organised.

This is how the game is introduced:

WELCOME TO THE

… a strange land, a fantastic land – a land where if Death doesn't actually lurk around every corner, he certainly has your home address and might drop in for the odd vindaloo now and again.

Based on Terry Pratchett's hilarious *Discworld* books, this game uses familiar characters and places from the *Discworld* stories to create an entirely new adventure. You will be controlling the actions of Rincewind – a none-too-successful Wizard from the 'Unseen University' in the city of Ankh-Morpork. Holder of B.Mgc – Failed, Rincewind's only real qualifications are an ability to sleep through the apocalypse, and a survival instinct honed by years of fleeing in abject terror from the slightest danger.

It's just one man and his luggage against the world. Granted, that world is pizza-shaped and is carried on the back of four giant elephants, which in turn stand on a meteor-pocked shell of a star turtle swimming serenely through space; granted, the 'one man' wears a tall, pointy hat and has a beard that smells like yesterday's breakfast – but still, the concept has a certain nobility about it, don't you think?

WORLD

You'll find here wizards, dragons, heroes and household hygiene specialists. There is danger here, but there is also custard around the place. Unfortunately, a dragon is now ravaging Ankh-Morpork, the world's leading city. Many people would consider this falls under the heading of civic improvement, but what Ankh-Morpork needs right now is a hero. All it's got, however, is Rincewind the Wizard, whose only talent is that he is not in fact dead yet ... and remember that a loaded pun sometimes goes off.

PREPARING

2. In *Discworld*, things that are exotic, serious or universal are suddenly undermined by here-and-now, daily-life words and ideas. With a partner, make a list of between three and eight examples of the **mock-heroic** from the game's introduction.

PRESENTING

3. On your own, produce a piece of writing explaining how each example works. Use a separate paragraph for each example. Try to define what **mock-heroic** technique he uses on each occasion.

You might find these paragraph openings useful:

★ Terry Pratchett takes traditionally impressive figures of fear and anxiety and gives them an everyday reality such as ...
★ He undermines all our traditional expectations of a hero ...
★ We are used to stories of one man's struggle against the odds, but not ...
★ He gives us a list of all the ingredients of a tale of exotic fantasy and then ends it ...
★ Two words used in a single sentence neatly sum up the unlikely combination of qualities in the story ...
★ The dramatic threat to the city is immediately undermined ...
★ Even his final joke shows elements of the heroic and comic ...

FOCUS FOCUS

UNIT 2

- *Study visuals from a computer game.*
- *Reinforce what you know about the mock-heroic.*

STARTING

1. The organisation of **computer games** relies a great deal on choices, which lead to interaction – physical or verbal – with other characters or creatures. The conversation below takes place after a number of other choices have been made, as you will see from the structure of the page opposite.

Sarcasm dialogue

RINCEWIND: (*Sarcastically*) So you're all the faculty heads – the giants of wizardry. This is it – this is as good as it gets.

DEAN: Contemplating promotion?

RINCEWIND: No, I'm contemplating a change of career.

Anger dialogue

RINCEWIND: (*Angrily*) Is this all you do all day? Just sit and make a public nuisance of yourself?

DEAN: I'm reserving my powers.

RINCEWIND: What powers?

DEAN: Well, for a start, I can read your mind.

RINCEWIND: (*Impressed*) Really? What do you see?

DEAN: Not much. You must have the 'big print' version.

UNSEEN UNIVERSITY

Structure

Unseen University

library   closet   arch-chancellor's room   kitchen   dining room   Rincewind's room

objects   people

carcass   food   staff   gong   lecturer   bursar   dean   Windle Poons   Senior Wrangler

dialogues

greeting   sarcasm   question   anger   goodbye

Words in red indicate a possible route through this stage of the game.

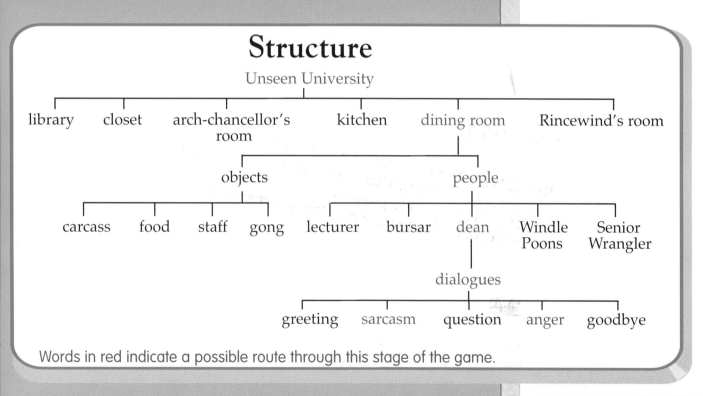

2. Discuss with a partner how the **structure** of the Unseen University enables the game-player to go through lots of stages and **dialogues**.

PREPARING

3. Look at the 'Anger' **dialogue** between the Dean and Rincewind. The job of Dean is usually that of an important, well-respected senior teacher at a university. Write down what you might expect him to say, in a more serious story, after the words 'I can read your mind.' Then note down what is surprising about what he does say.

- *Learn about the essential ingredients for computer narratives.*
- *Practise dialogues and other skills.*
- *Develop your own proposal for a computer narrative.*

DEVISING A COMPUTER NARRATIVE

STARTING

1. The programmers at Psygnosis chose Terry Pratchett's *Discworld* novels because they provided many of the essential elements of a **computer game**. The story within the game also had to have some clear ingredients – as listed below:

Genre

A **genre** is a type or **form** of story. There are many popular **genres** that work well in computer games: sci fi, fantasy, pirate, detective and so on. It can also be fun devising a new story pattern altogether. The **genre** for *Discworld* is comic fantasy.

Tone

The **tone** of a story will determine the reader's attitude to characters and events in that story. It may have a **tone** of high seriousness or of comedy. Even a comic **tone** can be subdivided into slapstick humour, **black comedy** (where we laugh at things we normally would not laugh at), angry **satire** and several other shades between. The **tone** of *Discworld* is comic **mock-heroic**.

Quest

A **quest** is a purpose or challenge for the **hero** of a story. It drives the **narrative** from beginning to end. It is one of the oldest forms of story dating back to Greek times. It is particularly appropriate to computer games, giving the player a clear motive when making decisions to advance the game. The **quest** in the *Discworld* game is to deal with the dragon attacking the city.

PREPARING

2. By now you should be reasonably clear about the **world**, the **hero** and his **quest**, and the **genre** and **tone** of *Discworld*. Now you are to devise a computer game. Write a brief introduction to the **world** of a game and its **hero** of your choice. Remember to make the **genre**, the **quest** and the **tone** clear. Remember your **hero** can be of either sex and of any personality you wish.

Language Pointers

- **'Black' comedy** is humour with a darker or more serious side, perhaps finding laughter in death or unhappiness.
- **Satire** is a form of writing which seeks to make fun of something, someone, or a story in a sharp and sometimes cruel way.

3. In order to develop your **narrative** you will need to develop other **characters**. There are **characters** apart from the **hero** and these are often found in **locations**. They add colour and often set challenges, providing clues or opportunities for the **hero** to succeed in the next stage of the **quest**. **Dialogue** between the **hero** and a **character** must work again through a series of choices. The writers must set out a **program**, taking into account all of these choices. In the *Discworld* game, Rincewind is offered a range of strategies and attitudes to choose from, such as 'Greet', 'Question', 'Say Good-bye' or respond with 'Sarcasm' or 'Anger'.

Territory

Computer games operate by making choices, like computers themselves. It is necessary to move the **hero** around a central platform or **territory** in which there are a series of clues to solve. Once the puzzle associated with that **territory** has been solved, the central **character** moves through to another **territory** and begins the next phase of the **quest**. The first **territory** of *Discworld* is the Unseen University. Typical examples of **territories** are castles, planets, towns and islands.

Location

Location is one of a range of places that can be visited within a particular **territory**. The **character** moves between places, each of them offering different clues and different assistance in following the **quest**. They also help to establish the **world** of the **game**. In the first **territory** of *Discworld*, the **locations** are **rooms**.

Objects

The finding, collecting and using of **objects** discovered in the various **locations** is a clear way of establishing for the computer that each stage or puzzle in the **quest** has been completed.

DEVISING A COMPUTER NARRATIVE

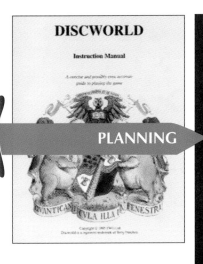

PLANNING

4. Create a set of **dialogues** between your **hero** and a character from one of your **locations**. You may like to give your **hero** a set of attitudes to take, as Rincewind has, like greeting, anger or question. Perform your **dialogues** with a partner to test how they would sound on screen.

5. Either on your own, in pairs, or in a group you are going to develop a **proposal** for a computer adventure game. This will be presented in the form of a cover sheet, introduction (such as the *Discworld* introduction you read earlier) and samples of all or some of the items from the checklist below. All your information will be in written form, but you may need to include drawings, or other images too. So far, you have written an introduction and invented a hero. Now, do the rest.

Item	Done
a **genre** – sci fi, fantasy, private eye	
a **tone** – **mock-heroic**, violent comic	
a **world** – a written introduction	✓
a **hero** – male, female or other	✓
a **quest**	
an initial **territory**	
a set of **locations**	
in some **locations**, a set of **objects**	
in some **locations**, characters	
for some **characters**, **dialogue programs**	
sample graphics for your prologue, **territories**, **locations**, **heroes** or **characters**	

PRESENTING

6. Present your work as stated above.

Poetry

● *Think about the use of the ellipsis.*
● *Identify types of future and conditional tenses.*
● *Express possibilities and ambitions in your own writing.*

Wishful thinking

STARTING

1. The beginning of this book focused on personal feelings and wishes expressed – or not expressed – through letters. The poems in this section deal with people coming to terms with who they are and what they want, like this boy being asked about his future by a teacher.

Grown up?

When I'm grown up?
What do I want to be?
Well, Sir,
Since you ask,
I wouldn't mind …
I wouldn't mind being a *tree*!
I'd like to push my feet
Into the soil,
And stand there
A few hundred years,
Just *being* …
Just being a tree.

But if I can't be a tree,
I think I'd just like to be *bad*.
I'd like to have cakes and champagne in the afternoon,
And eat condensed milk straight out of the tin,
With a green plastic spoon;
I'd have handmaidens bringing sherbet,
And a pet boa-constrictor called Herbert.
I'd lie on a silken divan,
Reading lurid novels;
And make fat profits,
From people in hovels;
I'd go to Oxford,
Take my teddy-bear,
And dine on oysters and paté,

Gin and jugged-hare.
I'd …
But he's not listening,
They never do …
One thing I'll *never* be,
When I grow up;
I'll *never* be,
A fat man,
In a pin-stripe suit,
Who smiles his fat smile,
At a pimply Second-Year,
Lays a heavy hand
On the boy's shoulder,
And says,

"Now, young man,
What do you want to be,
When you grow up?"

Then walks away,
Without listening,
With a sneer and a wink
At the Head,
And a burst of coarse laughter,
Down the corridor.

John Cunliffe

▶ **Language Pointers** ◀

Two ways of resolving uncertainty or possibility are:
● the **modal** form is when a **verb** is added to a main **verb** to show degree or **mood**. For example, 'I *might* go' is different from 'I *will* go'. The first shows uncertainty.
● **Ellipsis** marks are the dots used to create a pause – often in someone's thoughts or reflections.

PREPARING

2. Look at the poem. The poet has decided to use **ellipsis** marks in four places.

3. With a partner, read the poem again. Now discuss and write down your answers to the following:

   a. Why did the poet use **ellipsis** in each case?
   b. Does each one have the same effect?

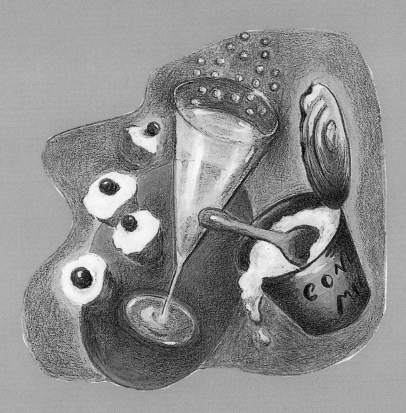

PLANNING

4. Discuss in pairs:
   a. The boy uses the **conditional** form 'I'd just *like* to be …' in the first part of the poem. Later, he says, 'I'll *never* be …'. Which of these two statements is more likely to happen?
   b. Why does the boy feel this way? How do the **verb** forms help him express himself?

PRESENTING

5. Write a set of horoscopes for each of the Zodiac signs. You will be writing about the **future**, and especially about the unknown. Select your **verbs** carefully, and think about your use of commas to split sentences, for example when using *if*.

41

- *Identify an archaic form of language.*
- *Write in the role of Lady Macbeth.*
- *Write a poem using verb tenses and adverbs of time.*

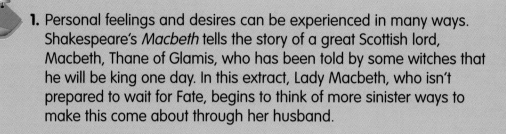

Ambitious thinking

STARTING

1. Personal feelings and desires can be experienced in many ways. Shakespeare's *Macbeth* tells the story of a great Scottish lord, Macbeth, Thane of Glamis, who has been told by some witches that he will be king one day. In this extract, Lady Macbeth, who isn't prepared to wait for Fate, begins to think of more sinister ways to make this come about through her husband.

Lady Macbeth:	Glamis thou art, and Cawdor; and shalt be
	What thou art promis'd. Yet do I fear thy nature;
	It is too full o' th' milk of human kindness
	To catch the nearest way. Thou wouldst be great;
	Art not without ambition, but without
	The illness should attend it. What thou wouldst highly,
	That wouldst thou holily; wouldst not play false,
	And yet wouldst wrongly win.
	Thou'dst have, great Glamis, that which cries
	'Thus thou must do' if thou have it;
	And that which rather thou dost fear to do
	Than wishest should be undone. Hie thee hither,
	That I may pour my spirits in thine ear,
	And chastise with the valour of my tongue
	All that impedes thee from the golden round
	Which fate and metaphysical aid doth seem
	To have thee crown'd withal.
	Enter a Messenger
	What is your tidings?
Messenger:	The King comes here tonight.

(Act I, Scene v)

Now note the points in the Language Pointers box.

- **Archaic form** – Lady Macbeth uses an **archaic form** of **tenses** here. She is talking about events which have not yet happened, and events she wishes to happen.
  thou art – you are   *thou wouldst* – you would/you would like
  thou'dst have – you'd have   *thou shalt be* – you shall/will be
- **Adverbs** – Rojada Ledge's poem uses **adverbs** of time, for example, *yesterday*, for organisation.

2. Working with a partner, translate the lines starting:
'Thou wouldst be great ... ' to ' ... wrongly win'.

PREPARING

3. Discuss how the news brought by the messenger will affect Lady Macbeth.

4. Write a short speech of about four lines by Lady Macbeth to the messenger, imitating Shakespeare's English, in which she tells him to prepare the King's room/chamber. Use as many of the **archaic verb** and **pronoun** ('thou/you') forms as you can.

5. Now read Rojada Ledge's poem:

Yesterday Today Tomorrow

Yesterday
we thought
the vote
would change
our lives

Today
we know
there's more
to power
than
voting

Tomorrow ...

Rojada Ledge

6. Think about who the 'we' in the poem refers to and what the subject of the poem is.

PLANNING

7. Now write your own poem using the same **structure**.
  a. Decide who will be the 'we' in your poem.
  b. Begin the first **verse** with 'Yesterday' and use the **past tense** to write about how things were.
  c. Begin the second **verse** with 'Today' and use the **present tense** to write about how things are now.
  d. Begin the last **verse** with 'Tomorrow' and write about how things might turn out in the **future**.

PRESENTING

Here is one possible subject:
- girls' football (*Yesterday we all stood on the touchlines enviously ...*).

FOCUS
FOCUS

UNIT 3

- Write a poem in the style of a given poet.
- Write a collaborative essay comparing two poems.

A sense of myself

STARTING

1. Poems can have similar, even identical, subject matter and yet be quite different in **tone**. Trying to identify this **tone** (or **mood**) is not always easy. The following two poems are very similar in subject matter but very different in **tone**.

At home

At fourteen I was not seen
by the others in my form
to be normal.
In a classroom debate
Jonathan Hawkins once created great laughter
by addressing us all
as ladies, gentlemen and Hegley.
But things were different
down behind the goal at Luton Town FC of a Saturday afternoon,
my pre-match chatter
mattered as much as anybody's,
belittling schooltime sniggers were no more
this was something bigger than schooltime
and at the entrance of the sacred twelve
swarming after their warm-up footballs
and soon to be put to the test
I was there with the rest
I was one of the crowd
I was part of the roar
LUTON
LUTON
LUTON
urging them to score,
and louder than Jonathan Hawkins.

John Hegley

▶ Language Pointers ◀

● The **tone** of a piece of writing is the expression of the author's feeling about a subject, for example, sad, angry, reflective, etc.
● The **mood** of a piece of writing is similar to the **tone** but is sometimes taken to mean the general atmosphere of the work.

I heard them say I'm ugly

I heard them say I'm ugly.
I hoped it wasn't true.
I looked into the mirror
To get a better view,
And certainly my face seemed
Uninteresting and sad
I wish that either it was good
Or else just very bad.

My eyes are green, my hair is straight,
My ears stick out, my nose
Has freckles on it all the year,
I'm skinny as a hose.
If only I could look as I
Imagine I might be.
Oh, all the crowds would turn and bow,
They don't – because I'm me.

Elizabeth Jennings

PREPARING

2. One way of describing the **tone** of a poem is by using a variety of **adjectives**. In pairs, discuss the two poems; looking particularly at the way the **mood** or **tone** of the poems changes from the beginning to the end.

3. Write down **adjectives** to describe the different parts of each poem: for example 'At home': lines 1–3: personal, chatty.
Use your own **adjectives** or ones from this selection:
humorous, sarcastic, serious, curious, resigned, happy, sincere, reflective, chatty, urgent, sad, excited, peaceful, confident, timid, victorious, proud, annoyed.

humorous?
sad?
sarcastic?
victorious?

A sense of myself

4. Write a poem expressing your feelings at this moment in your life. You must follow the rules below, and choose the style of either John Hegley or Elizabeth Jennings to get you started.

LANGUAGE DECISIONS

● Use the first person voice – 'I'.

● Compare the way you are with the way you would like to be, like John Hegley and Elizabeth Jennings.

● Think about the **tone** of your piece. Do you want it to be serious, sad, humorous … or something else?

● Make the last line or sentence particularly powerful.

Option 1. John Hegley's style

a. Write ten lines about yourself in a place where you feel awkward or unhappy. This will form the first part of your poem.

b. Now write ten lines about yourself in a place you like and where you feel comfortable and happy. Introduce this section with the line, '*But things were different...*'.

c. Write the last part of your poem about a situation which highlights how happy you can be compared with your sadness in the first section of the poem. Use a language effect such as **repetition**, or a shorter line, to show the difference from your earlier **mood**.

Language Pointer

● The **rhyme** scheme is the order, place and choice of **rhyming** sounds in a poem. For example, whether the **rhymes** are on alternate or consecutive lines, or follow some other pattern.

Option 2. Elizabeth Jennings' style

a. Write the first three lines of the poem using the **verse structure** as Elizabeth Jennings does:

- ● I heard
- ● I hoped
- ● I looked.

These lines should set up the idea that you are unhappy about something.

b. Begin the next section of the poem with the words 'I wish'. A wish might be for something small or something outrageous, but this part should show how you want to be different.

c. End your poem with two pairs of lines, the first beginning with the words 'If only'.

5. Finally, redraft and then copy out your poem neatly, paying attention to the Language Decisions box.

6. Comparing two poets

In pairs, jot down some notes in response to these points and then look at the lines of John Hegley's poem and Elizabeth Jennings' poem.

a. Which of the two writers is happier at the end of the poems? How do you know?
Identify the **rhyme** scheme: what effect does it have in each poem? (e.g. Why is there **rhyme** at the end of 'At home'?)

b. Note down any lines of personal emotion that draw you into the poems.

c. Which poet do you most sympathise with?

7. Now move into groups of four and write a short collaborative essay on the two poems, giving all your comments about the **tone** of each one. Start with a brief summary of the situation each poem tells us about. Use the notes you made in task 6.

FOCUS
FOCUS

UNIT 4

- Look at contrasting viewpoints.
- Look at verb forms in the present tense.
- Study verbs of movement.
- Write a comparison of the two poems.

For your eyes only

STARTING

1. Both poems on these pages continue the theme of strong, personal expression. The first one is about a woman at a party, watching the behaviour of her partner.

Manwatching

From across the party I watch you,
Watching her.
Do my possessive eyes
Imagine your silent messages?
I think not.
She looks across at you
And telegraphs her flirtatious reply.
I have come to recognize this code,
You are on intimate terms with this pretty stranger,
And there is nothing I can do,
My face is calm, expressionless,
But my eyes burn into your back.
While my insides shout with rage.
She weaves her way towards you,
Turning on a bewitching smile.
I can't see your face, but you are mesmerised I expect.
I can predict you: I know this scene so well,
Some acquaintance grabs your arm,
You turn and meet my accusing stare head on,
Her eyes follow yours, meet mine,
And then slide away, she understands,
She's not interested enough to compete.
It's over now.
She fades away, you drift towards me,
"I'm bored" you say, without a trace of guilt,
So we go.
Passing the girl in the hall
"Bye" I say frostily,
I suppose
You winked.

Georgia Garrett

PREPARING

2. In pairs, reread the poem and make a list of all the **verbs** of body or facial movement.

3. Select those **verbs** that refer only to the girl and discuss what they tell us about the girl's behaviour and character.

I Am Not That Woman

I am not that woman
selling you socks and shoes!
Remember me, I am the one you hid
in your walls of stone, while you roamed
free as the breeze, not knowing
that my voice cannot be smothered by stones.

I am the one you crushed
with the weight of custom and tradition
not knowing
that light cannot be hidden in the darkness.
Remember me,
I am the one in whose lap
you picked flowers
and planted thorns and embers
not knowing
that chains cannot smother my fragrance.

I am the woman
whom you bought and sold
in the name of my own chastity
not knowing
that I can walk on water
when I am drowning.

I am the one you married off
to get rid of a burden
not knowing
that a nation of captive minds
cannot be free.

I am the commodity you traded in,
my chastity, my motherhood, my loyalty.
Now it is time for me to flower free.
The woman on that poster,
half-naked, selling socks and shoes –
No, no, I am not that woman!

Kishwar Naheed

4. This poem also features the technique of the poet addressing the reader directly, although the subject matter is very different.

It is worth pointing out that it is the custom for many young people from Pakistan to have arranged marriages.

For your eyes only

5. 'Manwatching' uses the **present simple verb** form to create immediacy. It focuses on **verbs** of movement and facial expression. Now look at **verbs** in 'I Am Not That Woman'. Copy out and then add all the missing **verbs** and other words from the following lines of the poem:

> Verse one: I am the one you _____
> while you _____
>
> Verse two: I am the one you _____
> I am the one in whose lap
> you _____
> and _____ and embers
>
> Verse three: I am the woman
> whom you _____ and _____
>
> Verse four: I am the one you _____
>
> Verse five: I am the _____ you _____

6. Discuss in a small group:
   a. What do these individual **verbs** tell us about the relationship?
   b. Who do you think the poet is addressing?
   c. What evidence can you find?
   d. What sense do we get of that person from the **verbs**/lines you filled in?

Both poems

7. Discuss these possible reasons why the **audience** that the poets have chosen to address is 'you'.

   a. Although the poems are about personal situations, using 'you' also makes the reader aware that there are wider issues being raised.
   b. It draws the reader in, putting them in the shoes of the 'guilty' person.
   c. The poems are really meant for the 'you' of the poem, nobody else.

> **Language Pointer** ◀

- The use of the **present simple** (*I go, I see*) is often considered useful in terms of style in poetry, avoiding the **repetition** of 'ing' i.e. the **present continuous** (*I am going, I am seeing*).

8. Decide in your group which of the two poems is more hopeful, and note down the key lines that show this.

9. Imagine you were the boyfriend or husband in the first poem – or the 'you' in the second (whoever you think it is). Draft your own poem using the same basic **structure** as the original, but presenting the **viewpoint** of the 'you' character.

> PLANNING

10. Redraft your finished poem neatly, checking that you have retained the **verb structures**, kept the same pattern, and presented the alternative **viewpoint**.

> PRESENTING

11. Now look at the following picture of a young Indian woman. Discuss with a friend whether this is a 'traditional' or 'modern' image.

12. Discuss what 'expectations' your friends or members of your family have of you. Do they expect you to wear certain clothes or behave in a particular way? How do you feel about this?

13. Finally, write a comparison of the two poems, contrasting the two situations, the feelings of the poets and their expectations, saying which is the more hopeful. Use quotations to illustrate your points.

> FOLLOW-UP

FOCUS FOCUS

UNIT 5

- Learn what a CV is.
- Read a CV in the form of a poem.
- Select information from a poem for a purpose.
- Identify writing techniques.
- Write a personal CV poem.

A poetic CV

STARTING

1. Poets have always written about the lives they lead and they also use other forms of writing as frames for their ideas. Here Simon Armitage uses the idea of a **CV** (**curriculum vitae** – a record of your previous jobs that you give to an employer) to record his life.

CV

Started, textiles, night shift,
no wheels, bussed it,
bus missed, thumbed it,
in my office sunbeam,
    fluffed it.

Shoe-shine, gofer, caddie,
bellboy, three bags full sir,
busker, juggler, bookie's
    runner,
move along there.

Sweatshop, mop and bucket,
given brush, shop floor,
slipped up, clocked in
half stoned, shown door.

Backwoodsman number,
    joiner,
timber, lumber, trouble,
axe fell, sacked for prank
with spirit-level bubble.

Sales rep, basic training,
car, own boss, PA,
commission, targets,
stuff that, cards same day.

Grant, small hours, square
    eyes,
half-arse O.U. student;
painting job, Forth Bridge,
but made redundant.

Understudy, back legs panto
    horse,
put down, not suited;
broke in Dr Martens
for police force, elbowed,
    booted.

Big break: trap shut, kickback,
fall guy, front man,
verbal contract, public admin,
quango stunt man,

collar felt, fair cop, threw
    hands in,
covered tracks up,
mea culpa, coughed, took flak
for every lash-up,

shredded trash, dug out top
    brass,
ate crap, digested orders,
sat on facts, last post
took rap for PM's body odour;

rested, sick note,
self-certificated heart attack
but fit now, comeback,
job plan, welcome mat,

or out to grass, find door to
    lay me at.

Simon Armitage

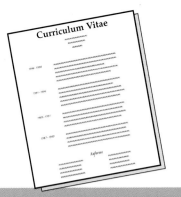

> **Language Pointers** ◀

- A **colloquialism** is usually taken to mean an informal phrase or expression that is used in a particular country or place, and can be difficult to understand for non-native speakers, for example, 'fluffed it'.
- **Formal language** is language used in a professional or business context, and is often viewed as 'polite'.

PREPARING

2. A real **CV** would have recorded his job as a 'bellboy/three bags full sir,' in the following way:

Hotel assistant: Charmouth Hotel (1998–1999)
Duties/responsibilities: aiding guests in porterage of baggage, assisting with their needs and requests.

However, the poem is written in a brisk, **colloquial** way. Copy out these phrases and replace them with more **formal** alternatives:

bussed it – took the bus/travelled by bus
thumbed it –
fluffed it –
sacked for prank –

PLANNING

3. You work at the Jobcentre where Simon Armitage has come to find employment. Copy and complete the form below and then use Simon's 'CV' poem to fill in as much as you can about his work experience. Use your imagination to add details such as names of companies and dates. Note that you will need to discard some information as unnecessary or unsuitable, and rephrase other pieces for the purposes of the form.

Work experience to date		
Job title	**Date**	**Duties, responsibilities and conditions**
Shoe-shiner Self-employed	Jan 1991 – May 1996	cleaning and polishing shoes
Textiles worker Hobbs Textiles Ltd	June 1996 – Jan '97	night shift

PRESENTING

5. Write your own full-length **CV** poem in an entertaining style, to include shortened lines, and other features from the original poem. Start by listing as many jobs as you can think of, both real and ridiculous.

4. Simon Armitage's poem is obviously written to entertain, and he uses a number of different techniques to amuse the reader. Find examples for each one of the techniques listed below:

stereotypes

ridiculous jobs

colloquial language

funny incidents

- Read a poem directed at a particular audience.
- Write a short poem in a prosaic style.

Will and testament

STARTING

1. Read the poem and use the Word Bank if you are struggling to understand any words.

Taking one **genre** – and mixing it with another – is something you will already be familiar with (for instance, when adverts use **verse**) but this is hardly new. The following will is in the form of a poem written by John Winstanley around the year 1700. It may or may not be close to what he really left for his wife on his death.

A Last Will and Testament

To my dear wife,
My joy and life,
I freely now do give her
　My whole estate,
　With all my plate,
Being just about to leave her.

A tub of soap,
A long cart-rope,
A frying pan and kettle;
　An ashes pail
　A threshing flail,
An iron wedge and beetle.

Two painted chairs,
Nine warden pears,
A large old dripping platter;
　The bed of hay,
　On which I lay,
An old saucepan for butter.

A little mug,
A two-quart jug,
A bottle full of brandy;
　A looking glass,
　To see your face,
You'll find it very handy.

A musket true
As ever flew,
A pound of shot, and wallet;
　A leather sash,
　My calabash,
My powder-horn, and bullet.

An old sword-blade,
A garden spade,
A hoe, a rake, a ladder,
　A wooden can,
　A close-stool pan,
A clyster-pipe, and bladder.

A greasy hat,
My old ram-cat,
A yard and half of linen;
　A pot of grease,
　A woollen fleece,
In order for your spinning.

An old black muff,
Some garden stuff,
A quantity of borage;
　Some devil's weed,
　And burdock seed,
To season well your porridge.

A chafing-dish,
With one salt fish,
If I am not mistaken;
　A leg of pork,
　A broken fork,
And half a flitch of bacon.

A spinning wheel,
One peck of meal;
A knife without a handle;
　A rusty lamp,
　Two quarts of samp,
And half a tallow candle.

My pouch and pipes,
Two oxen tripes,
An oaken dish well carved;
　My little dog,
　And spotted hog,
With two young pigs just starved.

This is my store,
I have no more,
I heartily do give it;
　My days are spun,
　My life is done,
And so I think to leave it.

John Winstanley

54

PREPARING

2. What the poet leaves his wife might tell us something about their life together. Copy and complete the table below, adding items from the poem to the appropriate column.

Practical	Unpleasant	Useless	Desirable

PLANNING

3. Now work in pairs and write out answers to the following:

- How many times does the man in the poem refer to his wife?
- What sort of life do you think the poet and his wife led?
- What does the character in the poem reveal about himself?
- Who is the **audience** for the poem? How do you know?

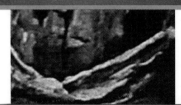

PRESENTING

4. Write a one-**verse** 'last will and testament' poem of your own. Keep John Winstanley's simple, almost matter-of-fact style. Of course, what is a 'desirable' gift for one person, may be 'useless' to another. Look at this example:

> *To my father, I leave*
> *My rusty skates*
> *These broken plates …*
> *A mouldy chocolate bar.*
> *A marker pen*
> *My puppy Len,*
> *My posters of the stars.*

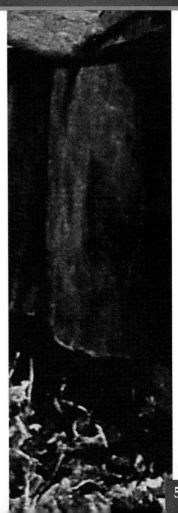

WORD BANK

flail – a tool for cutting corn
platter – a large flat plate
quart – two pints, or a vessel for two pints
calabash – the rind of a fruit, used as a cup
clyster-pipe – a pipe for relieving constipation
borage/burdock – hooked and bristly plants
chafing-dish – a container for keeping food warm
flitch – a joint of meat
samp – a porridge made with sweetcorn

● *Revise the use of similes.*
● *See how a poet conveys an intimate tone.*
● *Write a poem addressed directly to someone close.*

UNIT 2

An intimate tone

STARTING

1. Poetry has long been used to convey **intimate**, personal feelings, whether in pop songs, cards, or simply as poems sent privately from one person to another. Read the following extract from a poem and think about how it conveys a personal and close relationship.

Darling, this is goodbye. The words are
    ordinary
But love is rare. So let it go tenderly
as the sound of violins into silence.

Parting is sad for us, because something is
    over,
But for the thing we have ended, it is a
    beginning –
Let love go like a young bird flying from the
    nest,

Like a new star, airborne into the evening,
Watched out of sight, or let fall gently as a
    tear,
Let our love go out of the world, like the
    prayer for a soul's rest.

Let the roses go, that you fastened in my hair
One summer night in a garden, and the song
That we heard from another house, where a
    piano was playing;
The shadow a street lamp cast through the net of
    a curtain,
The river at night, smooth and silent Thames,
    flowing through London.
                    . . .
To you, once loved and for ever, from whom I part
Not because fate is blind, or the heart cold,
But because the world is neither yours nor mine,
Not even ourselves, not even what is dearest,
I offer what I can, my living moment,
My human span.

From 'Parting' by *Kathleen Raine*

► **Language Pointers** ◄

● When you are trying to describe the **tone** of a poem, or other text, the relationship between the poet and reader can be characterised as **intimate** (close) or perhaps have a colder, impersonal feel.
● Revision:
a **simile** is a comparison between two things, using words such as 'like' or 'as'. For example, 'Her eyes sparkled like jewels'.

PREPARING

2. The language of 'Parting' is quite different from that of John Winstanley's 'A Last Will and Testament' in the previous unit. For example, Kathleen Raine makes use of **simile**.
Copy out all the **similes** (comparisons that use 'like' or 'as') from the first three verses in this poem.

3. Write out the impression given by each **simile** you have listed. The first has been started for you:

> In the first **simile**, the 'end of love' is compared to 'violins into silence'. This gives a _____ impression of the love between the two people.
>
> In the second **simile**, _____ is compared to _____ (and so on).

PLANNING

4. This is an extremely personal poem and reads as if we are looking into someone's private world. How is this achieved?

● Work with a partner and list the words and phrases that help to make us feel we are observing an **intimate** relationship.

● Decide between you which are the two most **intimate** words, expressions or moments in the poem.

5. In the play *Cyrano de Bergerac*, a tongue-tied young man asks his friend, who has a way with words, to write romantic letters on his behalf to the woman he loves. Imagine a friend of yours asks you to do the same, or that your own girlfriend or boyfriend is disappointed with the letters you write and has complained about how boring and unromantic they are.

PRESENTING

Now write one of the following:

● A letter on your friend's behalf using the details below.
● Your own love poem to an imaginary or real boyfriend/girlfriend using the same **intimate tone** as Kathleen Raine's. Mention moments you've shared together and use **intimate**, loving language.

Friend's relationship: met him/her through another person; went shopping together; gave a particular present; first time he/she met parents.

> Rose Cottage
> Sandy Lane
> Hertford
> Herts
>
> 12th November
>
> My darling,
>
> I am just writing to say how wonderful it was to see you at the weekend.
>
> Thank you for the lovely flowers. I can hardly wait until the next time. Missing you already.
>
> With all my love,
>
> Juliet
>
> xxx

- Identify the characteristics of an ode.
- Examine extracts from two famous odes.
- Practise writing in the language of praise.
- Write an ode to a specific subject.

Singing praises

STARTING

1. An **ode** is a form of poem that was particularly popular during the nineteenth century. It often used 'flowery' language and was generally written for, or in praise of, an object or person. It was originally written to be sung and nearly always **rhymed**.

Gillian Allnutt's 'Ode' is a modern example, however, and is perhaps being used in a rather tongue-in-cheek way.

Ode

To depict a bicycle, you must first come to love it.
Alexander Block

I swear by every rule in the bicycle
owner's manual

that I love you, I, who have repeatedly,
painstakingly,

with accompanying declaration of despair,
tried to repair

you, to patch things up,
to maintain a workable relationship.

I have spent sleepless nights
in pondering your parts – those private

and those that all who walk the street
may look at –

wondering what makes you tick
over smoothly, or squeak.

O my trusty steed,
my rusty three-speed,

I would feed you the best oats
if oats

were applicable.
Only linseed oil

will do
to nourish you.

- Revising **personification**:
  If you use **personification** in writing, you give human characteristics to something **inanimate**, such as an object. For example, you might say: the wind *moaned* quietly, *chasing* the leaves across the grass.

I want
so much to paint

you,
midnight blue

mudgutter black
and standing as you do, ironic

at the rail
provided by the Council –

beautiful
the sun caught in your back wheel –

or at home in the hall, remarkable
among other bicycles,

your handlebars erect.
Allow me to depict

you thus. And though I can't do justice
to your true opinion of the surface

of the road –
put into words

the nice distinctions that you make
among the different sorts of tarmac –

still I'd like to set the record of our travels straight.
I'd have you know that

not with three-in-one
but with my own

heart's
spittle I anoint your moving parts.

Gillian Allnutt

2. This 'Ode' to a bicycle is a modern **ode**, but it contains many traditional features.
In pairs, find and write out an example of each of the following:

a. A phrase that describes a specific part of the bicycle in a romanticised way.

b. A pair of lines in which **personification** is used to give the bicycle human attributes.

c. A set of lines which includes a **rhyme**.

d. Any other pair of lines which demonstrates the poet's admiration and love for the bicycle.

Singing praises

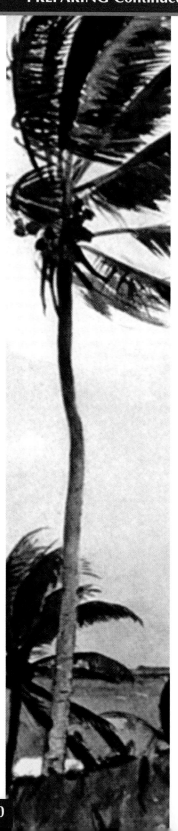

3. Earlier **odes**, as mentioned on the previous page, were often designed to be taken much more seriously, as the following extract shows:

> If I were a dead leaf thou mightest bear;
> If I were a swift cloud to fly with thee;
> A wave to pant beneath thy power, and share
>
> The impulse of thy strength, only less free
> Than thou, O uncontrollable! If even
> I were as in my boyhood, and could be
>
> The comrade of thy wanderings over Heaven,
> As then, when to outstrip thy skiey speed
> Scarce seemed a vision; – I would ne'er have striven
>
> As thus with thee in prayer my sore need.
> Oh, lift me as a wave, a leaf, a cloud!
> I fall upon the thorns of life! I bleed!
>
> A heavy weight of hours has chained and bowed
> One too like thee: tameless, and swift, and proud.
>
> From 'Ode to the West Wind' by *Percy Bysshe Shelley*

4. List all the words or phrases from 'Ode to the West Wind' which show Shelley's praise of the power of the west wind.

5. Shelley wants to travel with the west wind. What three things would he like to be that would enable him to do that?

6. In the last line, Shelley says that a 'heavy weight of hours has chained and bowed/One too like thee'. Who is 'chained and bowed'? Write down what it is that Shelley admires so much about the west wind.

▶ **Language Pointer** ◀

● As you have seen, **odes** often contain exaggerated praise for an object or being. A good example is this line by John Keats about an antique vase:

> Thou still unravished bride of quietness and slow time.

PLANNING

7. To become an **ode** writer you need to have something to praise. Choose a subject of your own, e.g. Ode to a Football, Ode to my Dad's Cooking, Ode to a Roller Skate.

8. Now decide who is telling the poem and what they are praising: for example a fisherman praising a salmon, an artist praising a famous painting.

Then brainstorm as many praiseworthy aspects of the admired 'thing' as possible, as in the example below:

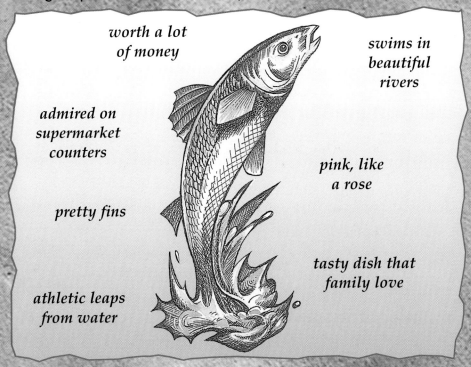

worth a lot of money

swims in beautiful rivers

admired on supermarket counters

pink, like a rose

pretty fins

tasty dish that family love

athletic leaps from water

PRESENTING

9. Choose one aspect and practise writing a long, 'flowery' description which is full of praise:

Oh, salmon – you who leap like a gymnast from silvery rivers!

10. Now write your full Ode to … (you choose a subject).

11. One of the most famous **odes** ever written is John Keats' 'Ode on a Grecian Urn'.

FOLLOW-UP

Find out what an 'Urn' is and what 'Grecian' means. Read the whole poem and find out what special qualities are being praised.

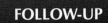

FOCUS FOCUS

UNIT 4

- Examine the traditional elements of a sonnet.
- Learn how to express a rhyme pattern in a poem.
- Learn about iambic pentameter.
- Write a sonnet and develop an argument.
- Annotate a sonnet correctly.

Sonnets

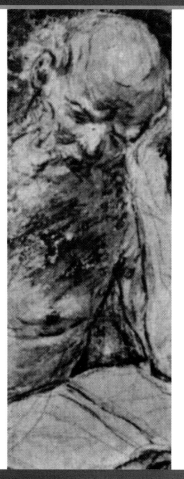

STARTING

1. Most of the poems on the preceding pages took a very definite shape or form. Each had a clear **audience**, or reader, in mind. One of the most common and widely-used forms of poetry is the **sonnet**. Shakespeare's **sonnets** remain some of the most famous ever written.

Sonnet No. 27

Weary with toil, I haste me to my bed,
The dear repose for limbs with travel tired;
But then begins a journey in my head,
To work my mind, when body's work's expired:
For then my thoughts, from far where I abide,
Intend a zealous pilgrimage to thee,
And keep my drooping eyelids open wide,
Looking on darkness which the blind do see:
Save that my soul's imaginary sight
Presents thy shadow to my sightless view,
Which like a jewel hung in ghastly night,
Makes black night beauteous and her old face new.
　　Lo, thus, by day my limbs, by night my mind,
　　For thee and for myself no quiet find.

William Shakespeare

PREPARING 1

2. The subject of this **sonnet** is a common one – being tired, but unable to sleep because of what's on your mind. However, the **sonnet** has a particular shape and arrangement. In groups of four, read the poem and then discuss the following questions and write down the answers.

　a. How many lines are there in the **sonnet**?
　b. How many syllables has each line got?
　c. In this type of **sonnet** which lines **rhyme**?
　d. Which words show that the **sonnet** is being addressed to a specific person?
　e. What is the poet's problem in the first **quatrain** (the first four lines)?
　f. What happens to the poet's thoughts in the second **quatrain**?
　g. What does the poet think he sees in the third **quatrain**?
　h. How does the poet feel at the end of the poem, in the last **rhyming couplet**?

> **Language Pointers** ◂

- If you **annotate** a piece of writing, you write over it, underline words or phrases, make notes around it, and so on.
- A **quatrain** is a four-line **stanza**, or part of a poem. Shakespeare's **quatrains**, **rhyming** 'abab', are sometimes called '**heroic quatrains**'.

The answers to these questions will have told you quite a lot about the **structure** of a **sonnet**.

PREPARING 1 Continued

3. Now see if you can put what you have learned into practice, by reading the **sonnet** below and then working through the exercises that follow.

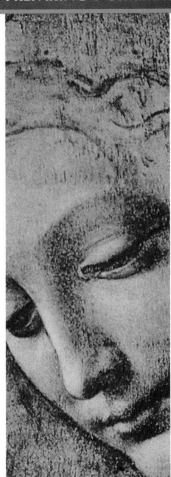

To His Mistress
Objecting to him neither toying or talking

You say I love not, 'cause I do not play
Still with your curls, and kiss the time away.
You blame me too, because I can't devise
Some sport, to please those babies in your eyes:
By Love's religion, I must here confess it,
The most I love, when I the least express it.
Small griefs find tongues: full casks are ever found
To give (if any, yet) but little sound.
Deep waters noiseless are; and this we know,
That chiding streams betray small depth below.
So when Love speechless is, she doth express
A depth of love, and that depth, bottomless.
Now since my love is tongueless, know me such,
Who speak but little, 'cause I love so much.

Robert Herrick

4. Copy out the **sonnet** and **annotate** it with the following labels:
- first **quatrain**, setting up the **argument**
- second **quatrain**, developing the idea
- third **quatrain**, developing the idea
- **rhyming couplet**, to conclude the **argument**
- key words signalling end of the **argument**.

PLANNING 1

5. As you will see, these two **sonnets** both follow a similar **structure**. Write about both **sonnets** and say what the '**argument**' (the poet's point) is in each, with examples.

PRESENTING 1

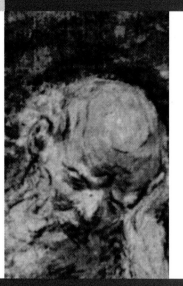

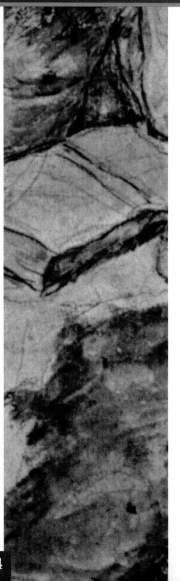

Sonnets

You will now know that traditional **sonnets**:

- are addressed to a specific **audience** (often 'you')
- use **quatrains** and a **rhyming couplet**
- have ten-syllable lines (usually **iambic pentameters**)
- contain a **viewpoint** or **persuasive argument**
- are finished neatly, wrapping up the **argument/viewpoint**.

PREPARING 2

6. **Sonnets** end with **rhyming couplets**. Here are three opening lines from **rhyming couplets** from three Shakespearean **sonnets**. Copy them out and add a second line to make three **rhyming couplets** of your own.

Remember:
- the two lines must **rhyme**
- the lines should have ten syllables each.

Don't worry if your second line doesn't make complete sense. Concentrate on getting the **rhyme** and **structure** right.

And yet, by heaven, I think my love is rare ...

But here's the joy: my friend and I are one ...

So long as men can breathe, or eyes can see ...

► **Language Pointers** ◄

● The term **argument** can be applied to a text to mean the view that is being conveyed by the writer. It does not mean 'argument' in the sense of conflict, necessarily.
● An **iambic pentameter** is a line of **verse**, usually of ten syllables, which contains five 'stresses', each generally falling on the second syllable of each word.

PREPARING 2 Continued

7. The following **quatrains** from three **sonnets** are missing two lines. Now see if you can copy and complete them. Again, don't worry too much if the meaning of your lines isn't quite right.

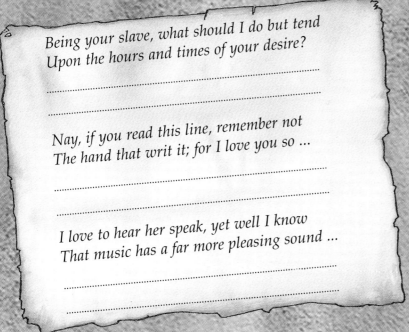

> Being your slave, what should I do but tend
> Upon the hours and times of your desire?
> ....
> ....
>
> Nay, if you read this line, remember not
> The hand that writ it; for I love you so ...
> ....
> ....
>
> I love to hear her speak, yet well I know
> That music has a far more pleasing sound ...
> ....
> ....

Remember to **rhyme** lines 1 and 3, and then lines 2 and 4.

PLANNING 2

8. You have practised the lines that form **sonnets**. Now it's time for the whole thing. Choose either of the following **arguments** as the basis of your **discourse** (discussion), or one of your own. Remember that you should address a specific **audience** in your **sonnet**, so adopt a **character** and write in that **role**.

● Recycling is better than rubbish (refuse collector to the homeowners he collects from).

● If you two-time someone you will suffer the consequences (boyfriend to girlfriend).

PRESENTING 2

9. Write your **sonnet**. If you are struggling to start, here is one possible beginning for you:

I know that you will blame me even 'though,
In life today our friendships come and go
I hurt you and ...

65

● *Learn about another form of sonnet.*
● *Use euphemisms.*
● *Write your own memorial poem.*

UNIT 5

Other sonnet forms

STARTING

1. The following poem by Christina Rossetti is also a **sonnet**, but does not quite follow the same pattern as those by Shakespeare. She uses a different **rhyme** scheme and the **argument** or point seems to be developed in two broad stages rather than four.

Remember

Remember me when I am gone away,
　　Gone far away into the silent land;
　　When you can no more hold me by the hand,
Nor I half turn to go yet turning stay.
Remember me when no more day by day
　　You tell me of our future that you planned:
　　Only remember me; you understand
It will be late to counsel then or pray.
Yet if you should forget me for a while
　　And afterwards remember, do not grieve:
　　For if the darkness and corruption leave
　　A vestige of the thoughts that once I had,
Better far you should forget and smile
Than that you should remember and be sad.

Christina Rossetti

PREPARING

2. In many ways, most of the language in the poem is straightforward, but to understand its point you need to identify the way the ideas are ordered.

   a. Work in pairs and discuss what you think the poet is talking about. At this stage your comments can be fairly broad (i.e. 'she seems happy or unhappy', and so on).

   b. Now, on your own, copy out the poem carefully.

   c. Label each line with 'a', 'b', 'c' or 'd' to show the end **rhymes** that occur. (Use 'a' for first **rhyme** sound *'away'*, 'b' for *'land'*, etc.)

3. Highlight the key word (at the start of a line) where the direction of the poet's ideas change and move from remembering to forgetting.

► **Language Pointers** ◄

● You use **euphemisms** when you wish to disguise or soften the impact of the truth, for example saying *I need to spend a penny*, instead of *I need the toilet*.
● A **refrain** is a line or phrase that a writer comes back to again and again, like a familiar melody in a piece of music.

PREPARING Continued

4. Now **annotate** the poem in a number of other ways:
   a. Underline or highlight **repetition** of certain words.
   b. Write comments alongside to explain or question certain ideas.
   c. Highlight lines or phrases that are particularly powerful – or difficult.

5. Re-join your partner, and compare the notes you have made. Try to reach agreement about the message or **argument** of the poem, the poet's situation and the story she is telling, making sure you refer to individual lines and words.

PLANNING

6. Christina Rossetti wrote:

   > Remember me when I am gone away,
   > Gone far away into the silent land …

   Discuss with your partner what the 'silent land' is.

7. You will probably have agreed that the 'silent land' has a far more common description – which the poet has chosen to ignore. This is called a **euphemism**. Below are a number of **euphemisms** which are used to replace the usual phrase or sentence.

   Write what the blunt truth is behind each **euphemism**:

   ● *I am terminating your ongoing employment with this company.*

   ● *She passed away.*

   ● *I need to make a quick visit to the ladies' room.*

   ● *Because you are follically challenged, I'm afraid that you are unsuitable for the job of hairdresser's model.*

   ● *The conflict resulted in a negative outcome for our soldiers.*

PRESENTING

8. You are about to leave school. What would you want your friends, enemies, teachers and so on to remember you for? Write a fourteen-line poem (in sonnet form if you wish) in which you use the **refrain** 'Remember me'.
   e.g. *Remember me for always being late …*
   Remember me for never handing homework in …

67

POETRY 3

FOCUS FOCUS

UNIT 1

- *Identify persuasive language and technical jargon.*
- *Identify poetic language.*
- *Make up your own 'cross-text' poem.*

Twisting poetry

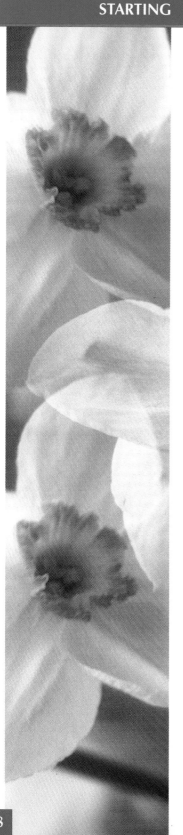

STARTING

1. In order to create unusual effects, or draw attention to a particular point, poets often make use of other types of writing (or other media). This is sometimes called **inter-textuality**. This poem cuts between one of the most famous poems in the English language and the **technical** and **persuasive language** of advertising.

The New, Fast, Automatic Daffodils
(New variation on Wordsworth's 'Daffodils')

I wandered lonely as
THE NEW, FAST DAFFODIL,
    FULLY AUTOMATIC
that floats on high o'er vales and hills
The Daffodil is generously dimensioned to accommodate four
    adult passengers
10,000 saw I at a glance
Nodding their new anatomically shaped heads in sprightly dance
Beside the lake beneath the trees
    in three bright modern colours
red, blue and pigskin
The Daffodil de luxe is equipped with a host of useful accessories
including windscreen wiper and washer with joint control
A Daffodil doubles the enjoyment of touring at home or abroad

in vacant or in pensive mood
SPECIFICATION:

Overall width	1.44m (57")
Overall height	1.38m (54.3")
Max. speed	105 km/hr (65 m.p.h.)
(also cruising speed)	

DAFFODIL
    RELIABLE – ECONOMICAL
DAFFODIL
    THE BLISS OF SOLITUDE
DAFFODIL
    The Variomatic Inward Eye
Travelling by Daffodil you can relax and enjoy every mile of
the journey.

Adrian Henri

▶ **Language Pointers** ◀

- **Inter-textuality** is the deliberate mixing of different types of **genre** or text to create a specific effect.
- **Technical language** is specialised language relating to a product or process.

PREPARING

2. Working in small groups, discuss which of the following points about the poem are accurate:

a. Both parts of the poem are selling something.

b. Henri is drawing attention to how silly poems about flowers are.

c. Henri wants to show how dull car advertisements are.

d. The point of the poem is simply to amuse us.

e. The poet wants to disturb us with some strange ideas and images.

3. Now, on your own, copy out and complete the table below by dividing the language of the poem into the three categories given as headings:

Poetic language from Wordsworth's original poem	Persuasive advertising language	Technical jargon (language specific to car manufacture and design)
I wandered lonely as	The new ... fast daffodil	fully automatic

PLANNING

4. It would be easy to say that the two types of writing in the poem – poetry of the nineteenth century and modern car commercials – are almost opposites of each other. However, look at this phrase from a car brochure:
Pure pleasure
Powerful, refined and with energy to burn
Agile and smooth
With grace and authority
More attainable than you ever dreamt.

5. Note down the similarities this shares with aspects of poetry.

PRESENTING

6. Choose any classic poem, preferably one praising a person or aspect of nature, and mix it with persuasive advertising or **technical language** for another product to create unusual effects (you needn't include all the words or lines from the original).

FOLLOW-UP

7. Note down at least two examples of adverts which use poetic techniques (such as **rhyme** or **alliteration**) to sell their products.

POETRY 3

FOCUS FOCUS

UNIT 2

- Compare two poems with the same title.
- Analyse the use of symbols.
- Write some short valentine's rhymes.
- Write your own valentine poem.

My phoney valentine

STARTING

1. Although poems are less visible than many other forms of text such as paperback novels, they often appear for certain special occasions, such as St Valentine's Day. Unfortunately, they can be rather sentimental. The poem below is not quite so conventional.

Valentine

Not a red rose or a satin heart.

I give you an onion.
It is a moon wrapped in brown paper.
It promises light
like the careful undressing of love.

Here.
It will blind you with tears
like a lover.
It will make your reflection
a wobbling photo of grief.

I am trying to be truthful.

Not a cute card or a kissogram.

I give you an onion.
Its fierce kiss will stay on your lips,
possessive and faithful
as we are,
for as long as we are.

Take it.
Its platinum loops shrink to a wedding-ring,
if you like.
Lethal.
Its scent will cling to your fingers,
cling to your knife.

Carol Ann Duffy

70

Language Pointer

- A **symbol** is an object or **image** being used to represent or carry strong meanings, for example, an apple to denote youth, freshness, health. However, people can also be **symbols**, for example, Nelson Mandela might be seen to represent justice and triumph over oppression.

Valentine

My heart has made its mind up
And I'm afraid it's you.
Whatever you've got lined up,
My heart has made its mind up
And if you can't be signed up
This year, next year will do.
My heart has made its mind up
And I'm afraid it's you.

Wendy Cope

PREPARING 1

2. Read both poems to yourself, or to a friend, making full use of the punctuation cues, and the pauses, or lack of them.

3. Wendy Cope's poem is relatively straightforward, but Carol Ann Duffy's is a serious attempt to say something meaningful about romantic **symbols** and Valentine's Day.

With a friend discuss and make notes on the following points:

a. Why is an onion more 'truthful' about love and relationships than a red rose or a satin heart?
b. What qualities does the onion have that make it a suitable gift?
c. What is the **mood** of the poets, judging from the **tone** and **pace** of the poems? (Are they angry? Reflective? Sad? Lonely?)
d. What sort of relationship do they have with the receiver of the valentine?

My phoney Valentine

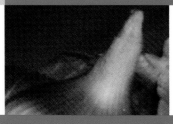

It seems obvious that the two poems are different, both in **form** and content, despite sharing the same title. But how do you put these differences into words?

PRESENTING 1

4. Write a short comparison of the two poems, using the words or phrases below as 'signposts' for your ideas:

- The first poem is about a woman who …
  while the second is about someone …
- The **symbol** for love in Carol Ann Duffy's poem is an onion, which shows us that …
- Wendy Cope's poem features a strong **rhyme** pattern which is similar to …
- The poem which sounds most like valentine card poems is …
  but the other doesn't because …

PREPARING 2

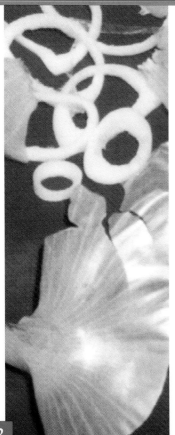

From early January, the shops are full of valentine's cards with messages which range from sloppy and romantic to funny and rude. Lots of them use traditional **symbols** for love, like a red rose, a pair of lips or a heart.

5. Brainstorm all the **symbols** and/or **images** we traditionally associate with love.

▶ **Language Pointer** ◀

● Wendy Cope's poem is a **triolet** – a poem of eight lines, with two **rhymes**. The first line is repeated in lines four and seven. The second line reappears in the last line.

PLANNING

6. Now draft some corny valentine's **rhymes** of your own. The examples below should give you an idea: if you're stuck, remember that roses, lips, hearts, doves, starry skies, kisses, birdsong and heaven are all good material.

> a. Roses are red,
>   Violets are blue,
>   Sweet Williams are sweet
>   And so are you.
>
> b. I love your lips
>   I love your nose
>   I love you from
>   Your head to your toes.
>
> c. In the palm of your hand
>   You hold my heart
>   Close your fist
>   And we'll never part.
>   Don't open your palm
>   Keep hold of my love
>   And I'll be as happy
>   As angels above.

7. Choose your 'best' (most corny) **rhyme** and compare it with a friend's. Which is the cornier of the two?

PRESENTING 2

8. Now write a more meaningful poem on the theme of relationships and love. You should either:

● imitate Carol Ann Duffy's poem, presenting an unusual valentine's gift which is **symbolic** of the relationship (a nettle? a glass?).

or:

● write a 'Love is ...' poem of ten lines, finishing each line with a strong, realistic **image** (e.g. *Love is a quick 'Hello' and then all day wishing you'd said something else*).

FOCUS FOCUS

UNIT 3

- Compare pop lyrics with conventional poetry.
- Annotate a favourite pop song.
- Write a pop song using pop conventions.

Is a song a poem?

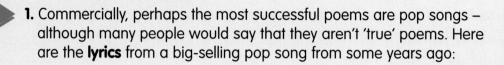

STARTING

1. Commercially, perhaps the most successful poems are pop songs – although many people would say that they aren't 'true' poems. Here are the **lyrics** from a big-selling pop song from some years ago:

Every Breath You Take

Every breath you take
Every move you make
Every bond you break
Every step you take
I'll be watching you

Every single day
Every word you say
Every game you play
Every night you stay
I'll be watching you

Oh can't you see
You belong to me
How my poor heart aches,
with every step you take

Every move you make
Every vow you break
Every smile you fake
Every claim you stake
I'll be watching you

Since you're gone I've been
lost without a trace
I dream at night I can only see
your face
I look around but it's you I
can't replace
I feel so cold that I long for
your embrace
I keep crying baby, baby please

Oh can't you see
You belong to me
How my poor heart aches,
with every step you take

Every move you make
Every vow you break
Every smile you fake
Every claim you stake
I'll be watching you

Every move you make
Every step you take
I'll be watching you
I'll be watching you
(Repeat verses to fade)

Sting

▶ **Language Pointers** ◀

● **Lyrics** are commonly understood as meaning '*the words of pop songs*'.
● **Lyric poetry** is the name given to a particular **style** of **verse** which presented a poet's feelings in a simple, direct way.

PREPARING

2. Some of the key features of poems are mentioned below. Discuss with a friend where they appear, and what poetic **form** they take, in 'Every Breath You Take':

a. repetition   **d. rhyme**
b. rhythm   **e. verse**
c. resolution (endings that explain or sum up key points).

3. Pop songs are generally addressed to 'you', particularly love songs. This song is no different, but is it a happy, 'lovey-dovey' song? Jot down any lines that suggest that this is a less pleasant, darker style of pop **lyric**, and add a comment about the relationship between the two people.

PLANNING

4. Here is your chance to show people that your favourite pop song is worth just as much attention as works by Shakespeare or Wordsworth.

Copy out the **lyrics** of your favourite pop song. Then **annotate** it using as many of the following terms as you can:

● **rhyme**   ● **verse**   ● **rhythm**   ● **resolution**
● **simile** ● **metaphor**   ● **imagery**   ● **repetition**.

PRESENTING

5. Display your **annotated** pop **lyric** in poster form, perhaps adding a short introduction saying why you like it.

FOLLOW-UP

6. You will have noticed that pop songs often have their own phrases and uses of language ('baby', 'cos' and so on). Write your own pop song (with or without music) using the typical language and **rhythms** of pop songs.

Typical situations:

> strong feelings of love

> meeting for the first time

> someone leaving

> someone breaking singer's heart

> ignoring advice from friends/family who say someone's wrong for you

> someone helping you become happy again.

- Write a series of poems for a specific audience.
- Use given information in poetry and magazine copy.
- Design and lay out a double-page spread from a magazine.

Poetry pages

STARTING

1. Poetry probably comes a poor second for many people behind more 'instant' forms of entertainment, but for others, poems are the only way to express what they want to say or read. Which of the comments below is closest to your own view of poetry?

> *I love reading poetry; I hated it at primary school, but since we've had to study it really closely, I've begun to see how it works ... why certain words sound good together ...*

> *Poems are just boring — some old bloke talking about flowers and love — not really me at all ...*

> *I write poems – but only for myself; they're a way of ... well ... saying what I want to say ... and sometimes I need only write a few lines – a few well-chosen words, often about who I'm going out with ... or how I feel about my parents ...*

> *Pop lyrics are OK ... they ought to be what we do at school ... some of them are really great — they'd be great without the music ... and there are poems that have been in films, like the one in 'Four Weddings and a Funeral' — that was OK.*

> *We're just not used to poetry – perhaps we'd be into it if there were more live performances with really good performers – but it'd have to be relevant to us – our lives – and fun as well as serious ...*

PREPARING

2. You are now going to 'sell' poetry to an audience your own age.

poetry?

song lyrics?

THE BRIEF

The editor of a magazine for teenagers has decided to do a double-page spread on poetry for next month's edition. The editor wants to have an alternative to the agony aunt and fashion pages, but it must still be lively and interesting. You've been asked, as a teenager, to come up with the content and ideas for the spread.

Language Pointer

● The job of the **Features Editor** on a magazine is to oversee any special topics or articles about one specific thing or issue, such as teenage pregnancy or attitudes to a new fashion, etc.

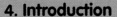

CONTENTS

3. The **Features Editor** has listed the possible content for each section under the headings below. Read through them carefully.

PREPARING Continued

4. Introduction

Introduce the page – what it's about – should be snappy, lively language 'selling' poetry.

5. Valentine poem

Make up your own, or write one using these ideas:

■ met at party   ■ danced once to a particular song
■ no name   ■ wore black   ■ left suddenly
■ no explanation.

6. Song spot

Put in your favourite **lyrics**

■ add reasons for choice   ■ key features of song/poetry
■ any background (e.g. on writer/singer).

7. Ode to a Star (**in memoriam** or adoration)

A poem about a favourite star or celebrity (dead or alive).

8. Advert

Use poetic techniques (**rhyme, alliteration**, etc.)

■ new drink   ■ lime   ■ best drunk ice-cold
■ no additives   ■ reduced sugar.

Stage 1

PLANNING

9. Now sketch out a basic page layout, showing where your articles will appear, how much room you are leaving for artwork, and so on.

Poetry pages

PLANNING Continued

 WRITING

Stage 2

10. Now, in rough (don't work straight into best) write the pieces in this order. If you're not sure what to do for each poem, look at the previous work on pages 70, 71 and 74 for inspiration.

- valentine poem
- song **lyrics** and explanation
- **ode** to a star
- advert using poetic ideas
- introduction
- other text (headings, captions, titles and so on).

PROOF READING

Stage 3

Proof read your finished pieces, especially for spellings, capitals and so on.

DESIGNING

Stage 4

Draw your design (based on the one you planned earlier).

LAYOUT

Stage 5

Copy your work into the appropriate places.

Stage 6

If there are awkward spaces left (most teenage magazines have lots of pictures as well as text), fill them in with either relevant snippets (jokey limericks) or **images**.

FINALISING CONTENT

PRESENTING

11. Once you have checked you've written the poems, introduction and articles in a lively, original manner, hand your finished spread into your teacher.

FOLLOW-UP

12. Research the life of St Valentine and write a brief article for the magazine, in the same lively style, on the saint who launched a million silly nicknames and messages.

Script & Speech

- Identify the difference between composed and natural speech.
- Learn about the dramatic qualities of natural speech.
- Write and perform a speech using formal and natural language.

UNIT 1

A personal audition

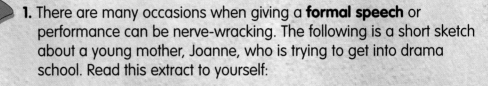

STARTING

1. There are many occasions when giving a **formal speech** or performance can be nerve-wracking. The following is a short sketch about a young mother, Joanne, who is trying to get into drama school. Read this extract to yourself:

Joanne walks nervously onto the stage. She has a text in her hand. She has come for an audition. The people she is auditioning for are sitting somewhere deep in the audience. She stands and waits nervously.

VOICE: When you're ready.

JOANNE: Oh. Right. Er well I'm doing a bit from the er ... 'Cherry Orchard'.
By Chekhov.
Silence.
I'm playing Ania, and it's er ... the speech at the end when she says goodbye to her mother ...
Silence.
Right then.
Joanne takes a final look at her lines. She puts the book face down (open at the relevant page), on a wooden chair beside her. Then she stands facing the audience with her eyes closed for several moments. She takes a deep breath and holds it. It appears at first as if she's preparing herself mentally but too much time passes. Finally ...
Oh no ... er ...
She quickly goes over to the chair, picks up the book and finds out what her opening line is.
Ah. Yes. Sorry about that. I'm OK now.
She puts the book down and is ready to start. She coughs nervously, and fidgets before finally starting.
'You'll come back soon, Mamma ... quite soon, won't you? I shall study and pass my exams at the high school and then I'll work and help you ...'
Silence. Joanne forgets the line again. She is starting to get upset. She closes her eyes again.
Sorry. Sorry. Sorry ...
She picks up the book, finds her line and puts the book back down again.
Shall I start again?
Silence.
I'll er ... start again.
She coughs again.
'You'll come back soon ... Mamma. Quite soon. Won't you? I shall study and pass my exams at the high school and then I'll work and help you.' We'll ... er ...' 'And-then-I'll-work-and-help-you. We'll – READ all sorts of books together. Mamma. Won't we?'
She stops. She is about to cry. She closes her eyes again.

- A **formal speech** is given for a specific occasion in which the purpose and **audience** are clear. For example, a **speech** by the best man at a wedding.

I'm sorry about this. Can I start again?
Silence. Joanne goes back to the book and looks at the text. But she begins to weep. Finally she sits on the chair and cries.

VOICE: (*Dismissing her*) Thank you.
But Joanne continues to sob gently. Finally she pulls herself together.

JOANNE: (*Quietly*) I know I haven't made a terribly good impression. But I can do better. It's just that I haven't been ... I just haven't been able to prepare for this because ... My daughter Zoe ... she's four, well she's been sick all week.
Pause.
I just haven't had time to ... to look at this (*waving the text*) at all. I'm sorry ... I'm wasting your time ...
Pause.
She spoils everything I do. She's been at home all week ... driving me mad ... wouldn't go to playschool. Temper tantrums all day, screaming all night and throwing up every hour. Sometimes I think I'll ... It's all I can do to stop her tearing the flat to pieces.
Pause.
That's all I've been doing for four years. Stuck at home, trying to bring up Zoe. I don't get any help. Her father has her on Sunday afternoons and spoils her rotten.
I can't be hard with her, because ...
I bath her and feed her and ... and dance for her and sing for her and ...
And pick up the food she drops, and apologise to the neighbours she swears at ...
And all she can do is tell me how much she loves her daddy because he buys her everything she wants.
All week she's been getting me to jump up and down on her new toy trampoline. It makes her laugh to see me looking so ... silly. 'Not now Zoe' I say. 'Mummy has to learn these lines ...' But she gets her way. I've been jumping up and down all week – on the trampoline Daddy bought her. If I tell her off she says she hates me. She says she'll stay at Daddy's house.
Pause.
It was daft me coming here. I thought Drama School might give me a way out. I'm sorry. I'll go now.

VOICE: Excellent. Very good. Best I've seen all week. We would love to take you. Run along now dear, to the registrar's office to sort out fees. We'll see you in September. Thank you. Next.

JOANNE: No no. That wasn't a ... a ... speech or anything. That was ...

VOICE: Sorry?

JOANNE: (*Finally*) It doesn't matter.
She exits. Returns. Picks up her book. Exits.

END

Peter Joucla

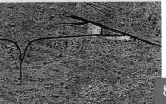

PREPARING

2. Now read the play script in pairs, taking turns to play Joanne. Make full use of the punctuation and stage directions given by the writer.

A personal auditon

3. With your partner, discuss the answers to the following questions:

    a. What part in what play is Joanne performing?

    b. Why is she having trouble remembering the lines?

    c. How can we tell when Joanne is speaking as herself, and when she's speaking lines from the play?

    d. Which **character** do you find more interesting – Joanne or the girl she's playing?

    e. How does she get on at the audition?

4. Now, as a pair, copy and complete the table, filling in what factual information we find out about the people mentioned in the script.

Ania (character in play)	**Joanne**	**Zoe**
lives with mother	single parent	Joanne's daughter

5. Look very closely at the way the writer has used language. In pairs, discuss and then write about the individual **vocabulary** choices the writer makes. How does he:

    a. show Joanne's distress with his use of stage directions?

    b. give a sense of her confusion and embarrassment through what she says?

    c. build up from her being embarrassed to her spilling out her feelings?

6. In the sketch, the 'voice' gives her a place at the drama school. He/she doesn't realise what Joanne said wasn't from a play. Write an audition report on Joanne as if you were the 'voice'. What impressed you about what she said? Use the form.

Melchester School of Performing Arts:
    Audition report

NAME:
Voice:
Movement:
Use of Space:
Facial Expression:
Gesture:
Understanding of Character:
Other Comments:

▶ Language Pointers ◀

- It is important that you use clear, well-chosen examples from the text when you are making a point:
  For example, the writer shows Joanne's distress with his stage direction *'She coughs nervously'*.
- **Natural speech** is **speech** that is unprepared – *ad lib* as it is sometimes called.
- **Vocabulary** is the range of possible words available to a speaker or writer.

PLANNING

7. With your partner, improvise a conversation about a disastrous morning (real or imagined), when you were about to go to school and everything seemed to go wrong.

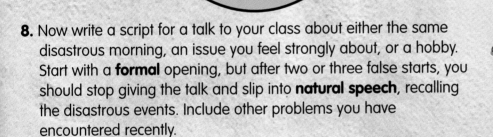

So, what went wrong then? How did it all start?

First of all, my alarm didn't go off. And then Mum forgot to check I hadn't overslept …

PRESENTING

8. Now write a script for a talk to your class about either the same disastrous morning, an issue you feel strongly about, or a hobby. Start with a **formal** opening, but after two or three false starts, you should stop giving the talk and slip into **natural speech**, recalling the disastrous events. Include other problems you have encountered recently.

This is being marked by your teacher and will go towards your exam grade.

LANGUAGE DECISIONS

- Consider how you will use punctuation, short sentences, **repetition** and so on to show your confusion as you move between **formal** and **natural speech**.

FOLLOW-UP

9. Perform your finished script to a friend or a group. Decide whether it conveys the difference between **natural speech** and the **formal language** of the talk.

FOCUS FOCUS

UNIT 2

- Look at features of three emotional speeches.
- Use these techniques to draft and make your own speech.
- Write an essay comparing the three speeches.

Let freedom ring

STARTING

1. The **speeches** on the following pages are very different from the one given by Joanne on pages 80–81. These have all survived as examples of great **speeches**. But why did they make such an impact?

Sojourner Truth was a former black slave who, when released, became a passionate campaigner for equal rights. Read this **speech**, given by her at the Akron Women's Rights Convention in 1852, and look at the **annotations**. It caused outrage among the white people present.

Ain't I a Woman?

rhetorical questions (ones which do not need or expect an answer)

personal references

repetition

religious reference

That man over there say a woman needs to be helped into carriages and lifted over ditches and to have the best place everywhere. Nobody ever helped me into carriages or over mud puddles or gives me a best place, and ain't I a woman? Look at me, look at my arm! I have plowed and planted and gathered into barns and no man could head me, and ain't I a woman? I could work as much and eat as much as a man – when I could get to it – and bear the lash as well, and ain't I a woman? I have born thirteen children and seen most all sold into slavery and when I cried out a mother's grief, none but Jesus heard me, and ain't I a woman? That little man in black there say a woman can't have as much rights as a man 'cause Christ wasn't a woman. Where did your Christ come from? From God and a woman! Man had nothing to do with him! If the first woman God ever made was strong enough to turn the world upside down all alone, together women ought to be able to turn it rightside up again.

pattern of three ideas

strong images

emotional appeal of children

▶ **Language Pointers** ◀

- A **rhetorical question** is one which expects only one answer and is used as a persuasive device, for example, 'We don't have to accept this, do we?'
- An **inaugural speech** is the one given at the official ceremony when a president or other newly appointed leader or officer takes office.

John F Kennedy, who was president of the USA and was assassinated in 1963, had an established reputation as a great speechmaker. Here are some extracts from his **inaugural speech**, made in January 1961:

> In your hands, my fellow citizens, more than mine, will rest the final success or failure of our cause.

> Now the trumpet summons us again … against the common enemies of man: tyranny, poverty, disease and war itself.

> The energy, the faith, the devotion which we bring to this endeavour, will light our country and all who serve it and the glow from that fire can truly light the world.

> And so my fellow Americans, ask not what your country can do for you … ask what you can do for your country. My fellow citizens of the world, ask not what America will do for you, but what together we can do for the freedom of man.

> Let us begin anew. Let us never negotiate out of fear. But let us never fear to negotiate.

> … pay any price, bear any burden, meet any hardship to assure the survival and the success of liberty.

> The torch has been passed to a new generation of Americans – born in this century.

> Let us go forth to lead the land we love, asking His blessing and His help, but knowing that here on earth, God's work must truly be our own.

2. Work in a small group. Reread the two **speeches**, taking a section or several sentences each. Discuss in what ways Kennedy's **speech** is similar in **style** to Sojourner Truth's.

PREPARING

Let freedom ring

3. The following **speech** by Martin Luther King was made to an audience of over 200 000 in 1963. It has become one of the most widely-quoted **speeches** in history. Read this extract carefully:

I have a dream that one day this nation will rise up and live out the true meaning of its creed: 'We hold these truths to be self-evident; that all men are created equal.'

5   I have a dream that one day on the red hills of Georgia the sons of former slaves and the sons of former slave owners will be able to sit down together at the table of brotherhood.

I have a dream that one day even the state of Mississippi, a state sweltering with the heat of injustice, sweltering with the heat of oppression will be transformed into an oasis of freedom and
10   justice.

I have a dream that my four little children will one day live in a nation where they will not be judged by the color of their skin but by the content of their character.

I have a dream today.

15   I have a dream that one day down in Alabama, with its vicious racists, with its governor's lips presently dripping with the words of interposition and nullification, will be transformed into a situation where little black boys and little black girls will be able to join hands with little white boys and little white girls as sisters
20   and brothers.

I have a dream today.

I have a dream that one day every valley shall be exalted, every hill and mountain shall be made low, the rough places will be made plains and the crooked places will be made straight and the
25   glory of the Lord shall be revealed, and all flesh shall see it together.

This is our hope. This is the faith that I go back to the South with. With this faith we will be able to hew out of the mountain of despair a stone of hope. With this faith we will be able to
30   transform the jangling discords of our nation into a beautiful symphony of brotherhood. With this faith we will be able to work

▶ **Language Pointer** ◀

● **Religious echoes:** When Martin Luther King gave this **speech**, many people called out in response. In much the same way, people cry 'Amen' at various points in a church service. This response to Martin Luther King's speech may have been partly due to his background as a preacher, and also due to the strong religious undertones and **style** of the **speech**.

together, to pray together, to struggle together, to go to jail together, to stand up for freedom together, knowing that we will be free one day.

35 This will be the day when all of God's children will be able to sing with new meaning:

> My country 'tis of thee
> Sweet land of liberty,
> Of thee I sing:
> Land where my fathers died,
> Land of the pilgrims' pride
> From every mountainside
> Let freedom ring.

And if America is to become a great nation, this must become true.
45 So let freedom ring from the prodigious hilltops of New Hampshire. Let freedom ring from the mighty mountains of New York. Let freedom ring from the heightening Alleghenies of Pennsylvania!

> Let freedom ring from the
>   snowcapped Rockies of Colorado!
> Let freedom ring from the
>   curvaceous slopes of California!
> But not only that: let freedom ring
>   from Stone Mountain of Georgia!
> Let freedom ring from Lockout
>   Mountain of Tennessee!
> Let freedom ring from every hill
>   and molehill of Mississippi.
> From every mountainside let
>   freedom ring.

60 When we let freedom ring, when we let it ring from every village and every hamlet, from every state and every city, we will be able to speed up that day when all of God's children, black men and white men, Jews and Gentiles, Protestants and Catholics, will be able to join hands and sing in the words of the old Negro spiritual, 'Free at
65 last! Thank God Almighty we are free at last!'

87

Let freedom ring

4. Now apply the **style** notes from Sojourner Truth's **speech** to Martin Luther King's. Copy and complete the table below and find one example of each **style** point to include.

Repetition	Religious reference	Emotional appeal of children	Strong images	Pattern of three ideas	Personal references	Rhetorical questions

5. On your own, note down which three phrases or sentences from the **speech** would have had the most impact, and explain why. Refer to the **techniques** already identified.

Martin Luther King uses at least one other device called 'opposing pairs' or **antithesis**.

For example:
"I have a dream that my four little children will one day … not be judged by the color of their skin but by the content of their character …"

6. Martin Luther King contrasts two situations here. Note down at least two other occasions in his **speech** when he uses the same **technique**.

▶ **Language Pointer** ◀

● **Antithesis** is the positioning of opposite ideas to create a specific effect. The use of **antithesis** is one **speech technique**, that is, a device for making a **speech** effective.

PLANNING

7. Now imagine you are standing for election to a school council which contains teachers, governors and two pupils from each year group. All candidates must prepare a **speech** to give to the members of your year. You have a free choice of subject. However, it should be something about which you feel strongly. Complete the following:

a. List possible topics (environment, school issues, rights of teenagers, laws, consumer issues).

b. Choose the one you feel most strongly about.

c. Note down ideas under the following headings:
● key points you want to make
● examples – especially ones that create images in your audience's mind.

d. Draft the **speech**. Write it out, almost without stopping at first, so that it has a strong, 'emotional' flow. Then, go through and look at ways you can bring in the skills and **techniques** used by the speakers in this unit.

laws?

environment?

school issues?

rights of teenagers

PRESENTING

8. Write the final version of your **speech** and present it to a small group or a class. Ask them to evaluate it.

Did you:

● make your point clearly?

● use some or all of the **techniques** you've studied?

● create clear **images**?

FOLLOW-UP

9. Write an essay in which you compare and contrast the effectiveness of the three **speeches** you have studied and say which would have impressed you most at the time.

- Look at a play adapted from a pre-twentieth century poem.
- Identify poetic techniques in a script, especially use of imagery.
- Script a poem for performance or reading.

UNIT 1

Scripting poems

STARTING

1. Dividing a poem into a script to be spoken by a number of voices is a useful way of bringing it to life. Michael Bogdanov dramatised Coleridge's *The Rime of the Ancient Mariner* which tells the story of a sailor who brings a terrible fate upon his ship when he kills an albatross.

In small groups (no more than five), read this extract from the original poem and then the play version by Michael Bogdanov (written in 1984).

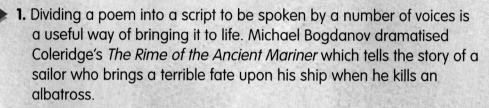

The fair breeze blew, the white foam flew,
The furrow followed free;
We were the first that ever burst
Into that silent sea.

Down dropt the breeze, the sails dropt down,
'Twas sad as sad could be;
And we did speak only to break
The silence of the sea!

All in a hot and copper sky,
The bloody Sun, at noon,
Right up above the mast did stand,
No bigger than the Moon.

Day after day, day after day,
We stuck, nor breath nor motion;
As idle as a painted ship
Upon a painted ocean.

Water, water, every where,
And all the boards did shrink;
Water, water, every where,
Nor any drop to drink.

The very deep did rot: Oh Christ!
That ever this should be!
Yea, slimy things did crawl with legs
Upon the slimy sea.

About, about, in reel and rout
The death-fires danced at night;
The water, like a witch's oils,
Burned green, and blue and white.

From The Rime of the Ancient Mariner by Samuel Taylor Coleridge

YOUNG MARINER:
The fair breeze blew, the white foam flew,
The furrow followed free;
We were the first that ever burst
Into that silent sea.

The MARINERS busy themselves, then gradually slow to halt.

ANCIENT MARINER:
Down dropt the breeze, the sails dropt down,
'Twas sad as sad could be;
And we did speak only to break

YOUNG MARINER:
The silence of the sea!

Plaintive pipe music. The MARINERS stretch out.

YOUNG MARINER:
All in a hot and copper sky,
The bloody Sun, at noon,
Right up above the mast did stand,
No bigger than the Moon.

Strange sound of boards creaking and high pitched whine.

ANCIENT MARINER:
Day after day, day after day,
We've stuck, nor breath nor motion;
As idle as a painted ship
Upon a painted ocean.
Water, water, everywhere,
And all the boards did shrink;

SAILOR 4:
Water, water, everywhere,
Nor any drop to drink.

ANCIENT MARINER:
The very deep did rot:

SAILOR 1:
Oh Christ!
That ever this should be!

SAILOR 2:
Yea, slimy things do crawl with legs
Upon the slimy sea,

Night and dancing lights.

ANCIENT MARINER:
About, about, in reel and rout
The death-fires danced at night;
The water, like a witch's oils,
Burned green, and blue and white.

Long silk ribbons snake in and out of a colour wheel, whirled by two members of the Company.

From *The Ancient Mariner* by Michael Bogdanov

2. Discuss in your group:
   a. What has Bogdanov added to the original poem?
   b. Has he edited or taken anything out?
   c. How has he kept the poetic **style**, yet made the poem seem closer to 'real' language?
   d. What staging difficulties would a theatre company have putting this on?

3. The poem partly works, as does the play version, because although many of these things – still waters, shooting an albatross, and so on – are difficult to show on stage, the strong **imagery** (the pictures the poet makes) makes it come to life. Now, in pairs, copy and complete the table below, adding any **images** from the poem and saying whether they are **similes** or **metaphors**.

Image	Type
hot and copper sky	(possibly) metaphor – can a sky be 'hot'?

Scripting poems

4. Now you have looked at how Michael Bogdanov did it, it's your turn. Read the next part of the poem; it tells of the Mariner's punishment and how a ship suddenly appears on the scene. It is worth pointing out that the sailor is only 'ancient' because he is telling this story as an older man much later on.

And some in dreams assured were
Of the Spirit that plagued us so;
Nine fathom deep he had followed us
From the land of mist and snow.

And every tongue, through utter drought,
Was withered at the root;
We could not speak, no more than if
We had been choked with soot.

Ah! Well-a-day! What evil looks
Had I from old and young!
Instead of the cross, the Albatross
About my neck was hung.

PART 111

There passed a weary time. Each throat
Was parched, and glazed each eye.
A weary time! A weary time!
How glazed each weary eye,
When looking westward, I beheld
A something in the sky.

At first it seemed a little speck,
And then it seemed a mist;
It moved and moved, and took at last
A certain shape, I wist.

A speck, a mist, a shape, I wist!
And still it neared and neared:
As if it dodged a water-sprite,
It plunged and tacked and veered.

With throats unslaked, with black lips baked,
We could nor laugh nor wail;
Through utter drought all dumb we stood!
I bit my arm, I sucked the blood,
And cried, A sail! A sail!

⟩ Language Pointer ⟨

● The ship that the Ancient Mariner sees is the 'Ship of Death'. It appears with two ghastly creatures on it who are gambling for the life of the crew.

5. On your own, script the poem for a number of different voices (up to five maximum, to include the Ancient Mariner). You may cut lines if you wish but make sure the strong **imagery** still comes across and that the story is still clear.

PLANNING

6. Either write your final version up neatly for presentation or return to your group and choose one script to perform. This can either be done as a straight 'rehearsed reading' or as a fully-fledged drama.

PRESENTING

7. Read the whole of *The Rime of the Ancient Mariner* and find out how the poem ends.

FOLLOW-UP

● *Look at imagery in the language of Shakespeare.*
● *Explore how images reflect the action of a play.*
● *Examine metaphor.*

Flowers and serpents

STARTING

1. The link between poetry and play is very strong. Shakespeare, in common with most of his contemporaries and predecessors, wrote in **verse** when it suited him and his language uses powerful **imagery** in a way that is consistent with that of individual poems.

In these selected lines from *Macbeth*, a play in which a Scottish lord murders his own king, Shakespeare uses strong **imagery**, in the form of **metaphor**, to show the audience the state of Macbeth's mind. Read each one and the situation in which the line is spoken.

… look like the innocent flower, but be the serpent under it. *(Act I, Scene v)*	*Lady Macbeth planning for the arrival of the King whom she and her husband aim to murder.*
O, full of scorpions is my mind … *(Act III, Scene ii)*	*Macbeth, seeing the ghost of a friend he has murdered.*
Life's but a walking shadow, a poor player That struts and frets his hour upon the stage … *(Act V, Scene v)*	*Macbeth finding out his wife has killed herself.*
They have tied me to a stake. I cannot fly … *(Act V, Scene vii)*	*Macbeth finding out his castle is surrounded …*

PREPARING

2. In pairs, agree on what you think each of these **metaphors** tells us about the way Macbeth and his wife are thinking.

PLANNING

3. We can do a similar exercise with another of Shakespeare's characters, Hamlet. During the play that bears his name, he discovers that his uncle murdered his father and married his mother. Hamlet at first suspects, and is then told by the ghost of his father what happened. Look at the uses of **metaphor** from the play on the page opposite. Alongside them are the occasions when they are spoken in the play, jumbled into the wrong order.

a. O that this too too solid flesh would melt,
Thaw, and resolve itself into a dew …
(Act I, Scene ii)

i Hamlet is unsure how to act, whether it's better to suffer silently, or to act violently.

b. Whether 'tis nobler in the mind to suffer
The slings and arrows of outrageous fortune,
Or to take arms against a sea of troubles …
(Act III, Scene i)

ii Hamlet warns two men sent to spy on him that he knows they're trying to find out his plans.

c. Be thou as chaste as ice, as pure as snow,
thou shalt not escape calumny …
(Act III, Scene ii)

iii After having been forced to meet with his uncle and mother publicly, Hamlet feels that he wants to die.

d. You would play upon me, you would seem to know my stops, you would pluck out the heart of my mystery …
(Act III, Scene ii)

iv Fortinbras, the new King to be, arrives at the end of the play to find the dead bodies of Hamlet, his mother, Ophelia's brother, and the King (Hamlet's uncle) and wonders what has happened.

e. I will speak daggers to her, but use none.
(Act III, Scene ii)

v Hamlet warns the woman he once said he loved that however good she is she cannot escape the evil of the world.

f. O proud death,
What feast is toward …
(Act V, Scene ii)

vi Hamlet plans to confront his mother with the truth about his murderous uncle – but he won't physically harm her.

4. Look at each quotation (left-hand column) and link it to the moment in the play (right-hand column) when you think it occurred. Then, note alongside what you think the main emotion being felt by the speaker is on each occasion.

PLANNING Continued

5. Copy and complete the following table using **metaphors**. Avoid **clichés** and make your lines as vivid and original as possible.

PRESENTING

Emotion	Metaphor
confusion	*My head is a tangle of …*
despair	*My mind is an ocean of …*
happiness	*My heart is …*
fear	*My pulse is …*
jealousy	*My thoughts are …*

FOCUS FOCUS

- Identify and use humour through language.
- Understand the effectiveness of rhythm and rhyme.
- Write and perform a speech using dramatic humour.

UNIT 3

French insults

STARTING

1. Dramatic humour requires its own specific language. In *Cyrano de Bergerac*, the hero, a French swordsman-poet who has an enormous nose, uses great dexterity of language to mock someone who has, rather stupidly, told him his nose is 'large'. Cyrano wonders if the man couldn't have found a better insult.

Nothing more?
Just a fatuous smirk? Oh, come, there are fifty-score
Varieties of comment you could find
If you possessed a modicum of mind.
For instance, there's the frank aggressive kind:
'If mine achieved that hypertrophic state,
I'd call a surgeon in to amputate.'
The friendly: 'It must dip into your cup.
You need a nasal crane to hoist it up.'
The pure descriptive: 'From its size and shape,
I'd say it was a rock, a bluff, a cape –
No, a peninsula – how picturesque!'
The curious: 'What's that? A writing desk?'
The gracious: 'Are you fond of birds? How sweet –
A Gothic perch to rest their tiny feet.'
The truculent: 'You a smoker? I suppose
The fumes must gush out fiercely from that nose
And people think a chimney is on fire.'
Considerate: 'It will drag you in the mire
Head first, the weight that's concentrated there.
Walk carefully.' The tender-hearted swear
They'll have a miniature umbrella made
To keep the rain off; or, for summer shade.
Then comes the pedant: 'Let me see it, please.
That mythic beast of Aristophanes,

The hippocampocamelelephunt,
Had flesh and bone like that stuck up in front.'
Insolent: 'Quite a useful gadget, that.
You hold it high and then hang up your hat.'
Emphatic: 'No fierce wind from near or far,
Save the mistral, could give that nose catarrh.'
Impressed: 'A sign for a perfumery!'
Dramatic: 'When it bleeds, it's the Red Sea.'
Lyric, 'Ah, Triton rising from the waters,
Honking his wretched conch at Neptune's daughters.'
Naïve: 'How much to view the monument?'
Speculative: 'Tell me, what's the rent
For each or both of those unfurnished flats?'
Rustic: 'Nay, Jarge, that ain't no nose. Why, that's
A giant turnip or a midget marrow.
Let's dig it up and load it on the barrow.'
The warlike: 'Train it on the enemy!'
Practical: 'Put that in a lottery
For noses; and it's bound to win first prize.'

From *Cyrano de Bergerac* by *Edmond Rostand* (from a translation by Anthony Burgess)

▶ Language Pointer ◀

● In a long **speech** such as Cyrano's, it is important that you give each line – or insult in this case – its own voice, varying the **pace**, **pitch** and emphasis.

PREPARING

2. Check you understand all the **vocabulary** then answer these questions:
  ● Which is the most amusing insult in the **speech**?
  ● Which creates the best picture?
  ● Which is the most insulting?

3. This speech is given with a crowd of onlookers present. Note down how Cyrano proves his cleverness and wit here. Think particularly about the fact that he's **rhyming** each insult and at whom the insults are directed.

4. Practise giving Cyrano's **speech**, adopting a different voice, or **accent**, to fit each of the insults.

PRESENTING

5. Perform the **speech**, preferably to a group of onlookers, in as dramatic a fashion as possible.

6. Create your own 'self-insulting' **speech**, either based on a feature about yourself you don't like, or rewriting Cyrano's **speech**, adding some new lines about his nose. Remember to preface each one with the category of insult (e.g. 'dramatic') and try to imitate the **rhythm** and **rhyme** where possible.

FOLLOW-UP

7. Find out what happens in the original play. There is also a modern version, made into a film called *Roxanne*, although this includes several changes to the original story.

- Consider interpretations of a scene from 'Macbeth'.
- Perform the scene in different ways.
- Work as a director.
- Summarise your thoughts in a director's notebook.

New direction

STARTING

1. Directors of plays need a firm grasp not only of what happens in a play but also of the way they want actors and actresses to **interpret** the main **roles**. The following extract is also from *Macbeth* (see page 94). Here Macbeth and his wife are discussing the possible murder of the king.

1–5: Macbeth says he won't go through with the murder – says the King has spoken well of him recently.

MACBETH
We will proceed no further in this business.
He hath honoured me of late, and I have bought
Golden opinions from all sorts of people,
Which would be worn now in their newest gloss,
Not cast aside so soon.

5 LADY MACBETH
Was the hope drunk
Wherein you dressed yourself? Hath it slept since?
And wakes it now to look so green and pale

6–16: Lady Macbeth asks whether Macbeth had been 'pretending' when he'd spoken before about the killing – or whether he's a coward.

At what it did so freely? From this time
10 Such I account thy love. Art thou afeard
To be the same in thine own act and valour
As thou art in desire? Wouldst thou have that
Which thou esteem'st the ornament of life,
And live a coward in thine own esteem,
Letting 'I dare not' wait upon 'I would,'
15 Like the poor cat i'th'adage?

17–19: Macbeth says he's as brave as any man.

MACBETH
Prithee, peace.
I dare do all that may become a man;
Who dares do more is none.

20–32: She says he's only a man if he goes through with it; she'd have done it herself if she'd promised, as he did.

LADY MACBETH
What beast was't then
21 That made you break this enterprise to me?
When you durst do it, then you were a man;
And to be more than what you were, you would
Be so much more the man. Nor time nor place
25 Did then adhere, and yet you would make both.
They have made themselves, and that their fitness now
Does unmake you. I have given suck, and now
How tender 'tis to love the babe that milks me.
I would, while it was smiling in my face,
Have plucked my nipple from his boneless gums
30 And dashed the brains out, had I so sworn
As you have done to this.

MACBETH
If we should fail?
LADY MACBETH
We fail?
35 But screw your courage to the sticking-place,
And we'll not fail.

(*Act 1, Scene VII*)

2. Working in pairs, discuss:
   a. your initial feelings about the way Macbeth and his wife are speaking to each other.
   b. key phrases or lines in the **speech** that actors should focus on.

3. Now perform the scene in four different ways. For each performance you will need to try out some simple movements, perhaps one of you sitting, the other standing, or standing at arm's length, and so on.

Performance 1:
Lady Macbeth: angry
Macbeth: apologetic/timid

Performance 2:
Lady Macbeth: mocking/half-joking
Macbeth: serious/determined

Performance 3:
Lady Macbeth: tense/irritated
Macbeth: joking/pretending he's not going to go ahead

Performance 4:
You decide the **interpretation**

Discuss which version was:

most convincing

most interesting

4. Many directors keep notebooks during rehearsals, or record their thoughts later on. Write a full account of how you think this scene should be played. Include details under the following headings:

a. A brief summary of the scene.
b. How the actor and actress should **interpret** the roles.
c. How they should move and speak at various times in the scene (an **annotated** version of the scene would help here).
d. How **pace** and **rhythm** can be used.

FOCUS
FOCUS

UNIT 1

- Identify features of a film screenplay.
- Study and write in the style of juxtaposition.
- Use descriptions of film images to create script.
- Respond appropriately to a given atmosphere.

Images in action

STARTING

1. Films convey **mood** or atmosphere primarily through real, rather than word **images** although language is still fundamental. A film **screenplay** has to describe these real **images** clearly. Read this **description** of the opening shots of the film *Don't Look Now*, adapted from a story by Daphne du Maurier.

Titles

A series of stylised images – Escher, Magritte – that are disturbing, disorientating. Figures, insects, impossible buildings, reflected images. All should convey a sense of foreboding – of things not being as they seem. A momentary impression of a small, distorted, gargoyle-like creature. Vivid red. And then a strange, reflective pond of water that ripples and sears in the mind a moment.

DISSOLVE TO
1. Ext. A field, Suffolk, day

High summer, the ground bleached by sun, deep country. A GIRL plays in the glade beside the field. She wears a pretty dress and moves with inborn grace.

The GIRL is barely five. She is delicate, laughing, happy on this fine day in a perfect setting.

She plays with an ACTION-MAN doll, strangely at odds with the prettiness of the situation and herself. The doll emits instruction in a thin, mechanical voice, as she pulls on its recording wire.

ACTION-MAN Action-Man patrol, fall in! Hold your fire until I give the order.

The GIRL and the ACTION-MAN are lying among the tangled roots of a beech tree. The ersatz masculinity of the recorded voice is muffled as the doll lies on its stomach beside the GIRL, the green visor over its eyes reflecting the GIRL's face. A little way away from them is the object of their attack – a little wooden fort, hopelessly out of scale. The ACTION-MAN will be a giant when he captures it.

ACTION-MAN Mortar attack! Dig in!

> **Language Pointer** <

● **Juxtaposition** is the placing of two things – ideas, words, **images**
and so on – close together. In film, this is usually done in order to
create a specific effect, such as humour, suspense or surprise.

*There is a house some two hundred yards from where the little GIRL
plays. The house stands on its own, slightly elevated. It is old, restored
well but not expensively, with the garden still unformed and moving
from the overgrown grass space beside the walls of the house to a wild
tangle as it merges with the woodland area beyond.*

2. Ext. Outside a house in Suffolk, day
*A boy, JOHNNY, about eleven years old, rattles away from the house
on his bicycle. He rides bumping down to the narrow track in the
woodland towards where his sister plays. A loose spoke clicks.*
  *As he disappears into the woodland the CAMERA RISES slightly
and, for the first time, we recognise the curious absence of any bird
song. The reason is quickly apparent: the woodland is occupied by
rooks. Their empty caw-cawing as they wheel and settle, black,
hunched figures, keeping to the tips of the trees, gives a sudden sense
of strangeness to this landscape.*

3. Ext. Woodland beyond house, day
*JOHNNY's bicycle comes down the narrow woodland path and quite
suddenly a pane of glass that we had not seen before lying in the path
is shattered into a thousand fragments as the bicycle wheel goes over it.*

2. A feeling of unease is created in this opening through the
juxtaposition of certain **images/descriptions**:

e.g. *boy cycling in countryside* (represents freedom/childhood)
loose spoke on bike (represents?)

With a friend list any other examples of **juxtapositions** such as this,
and any other details that suggest unease or that something
unpleasant is about to occur.

PREPARING

WORD BANK

ersatz – cheaper or poorer alternative
to the real thing
gargoyle – a grotesque carved face or
figure often found on church buildings

Images in action

PLANNING

Unless we have actually seen the film before, it is, of course, impossible to say what will happen next. However, the information we have been given in visual and **linguistic** clues suggests worse is to come, despite the otherwise idyllic scene.

3. Now, on your own, jot down details of the next four scenes. This can be done in a relatively simple way as shown:

Scene 1: We see Johnny falling from his bike in slow motion with the rooks circling overhead.

Sketch your ideas for each shot in a series of four boxes like the one below.

4. Once you have finished, you are ready to turn your ideas into a **screenplay** like the original you have studied.

Go back and look at the layout of the original. Then **draft**, in writing, your four shots or scenes into separate descriptions in the manner of the real script. You need only describe what the camera sees and whether it's an exterior or interior **setting**.

> **Language Pointers** ◀

The following characteristics are common to **screenplays**:
- Descriptions of **setting** are often in a series of list-like, almost incomplete sentences: for example, High summer, the ground bleached and so on.
- EXT./INT. is used to denote **exterior** (outside) and **interior** (inside).
- Clear, focused detail: for example, the Action-Man doll which 'emits instructions in a thin mechanical voice'.

PRESENTING

5. Copy out your **screenplay** scenes neatly with clear headings and numberings for the scenes.

One of the techniques used to show unease, or something threatening, in a film is the use of lighting. Look at the photo below. How is lighting used? What does it tell us about the people in the light?

FOLLOW-UP

6. Juxtaposition

Write a detailed prose **description** of a room being entered by someone (perhaps a detective) in which everything seems to be of a particular **style** but within which there is at least one single object which is out of place). For example: a dirty, messy bedsit with one single, beautifully kept carving from Africa.

FOCUS FOCUS

UNIT 2

- Understand and use technical terms for filming and compare camera shots.
- Draw a layout sheet from a film script.
- Write the opening of a film script.

Much ado

STARTING

1. Film-makers have to think visually; if they are working from an existing story or play they need to look for the potential in the words, particularly at the beginning. Read the opening of Shakespeare's *Much Ado About Nothing*.

ACT 1   SCENE 1
Messina   Leonato's house

Enter LEONATO, governor of Messina, HERO his daughter, and BEATRICE his niece, with a MESSENGER

LEONATO   I learn in this letter that Don Pedro of Aragon comes this night to Messina.

MESSENGER   He is very near by this. He was not three leagues off when I left him.

What do we find out from this? Simply that:

- Don Pedro is soon to be arriving in Messina.
- Leonato has received a letter about it – so it's a message for him.
- There is little time left.

At first glance this does not appear to be a promising start to a film. Kenneth Brannagh, however, realised its potential and transformed it into this:

Exterior/**PICNIC SITE**/Day

A misty watercolour painting which fills the entire frame. It is a view of LEONATO'S VILLA. Nesting on top of the hillside, it sits alone, away from Messina itself. Looking more like a rather grand, expansive farmhouse, it suns itself in the beauty of the autumnal late afternoon. The painting shows us the villa's rather crumbling grandeur: the orchard behind, the formal garden to the side, the little chapel, and here and there the farm workers occupied in tending to this self-contained rural Italian paradise. We have dwelt on the painting but a moment until the group laughter has subsided. As it does the VOICE OFFSCREEN begins again. The sounds of the country and a light, as yet distant, musical Air fills the soundtrack as we PAN left to reveal ...

▶ **Language Pointer** ◀

● The **technical terms** of film-making are those words and phrases which are usually connected with the actual process of shooting the film. **Exterior**, for example, is the accepted term denoting an outside **location**.

PREPARING

2. To understand what Kenneth Brannagh did, you need to look first at the **technical language** on your own – list any such language, **technical terms** (like '**exterior**') or ways the script is set out.

3. Now read the next few pages in the film script:

A great cloud of dust heralds the imminent arrival of Horsemen. As one, LEONATO, HERO, MARGARET, URSULA, BEATRICE, THE MESSENGER, THE DONKEY and the OTHER SERVANTS start to make down the hillside to reach the Villa in time to welcome their guests. As we watch their manic retreat, we hear, screamed,

MESSENGER:
Don Pedro is approaching!

The CREDITS begin to roll over the following sequence of rapid intercutting between the men and the women. Drums will lead us into the full orchestral accompaniment. The mood is glorious, celebratory, fun!

Exterior/**DIRT ROAD**/Day

Road and sky and heat haze. All we can hear is the drumming of hooves. The flutter of two flags appears, over the crest of the road. CUT.

Exterior/**HILLSIDE**/Day

Wide shot looking up at the top of the hill. A moment of silence before, Geronimo-like, all the women and other picnickers surge over the top towards us. We CUT in to see each individual CLOSE, as they bound down the hill. A mixture of REAL TIME and SLOW MOTION.

Exterior/**DIRT ROAD**/Day

CLOSE on horses' hooves and rippling horseflesh. A mixture of REAL TIME and SLOW MOTION. CUT.

Exterior/**DIRT ROAD**/Day

At last, over the brow of the road, fully revealed, are DON PEDRO and his men. Riding through a mist of dust and heat haze, they look like a combination of Omar Sharif riding into Lawrence of Arabia and The Magnificent Seven. They ride abreast spanning the width of the road and our screen. With tight leather trousers and boots, a mixture of sweaty shirts and military jackets, they canter in uniform rhythm as one beast.

(Continued on
page 106.)

105

Much ado

(Continued from page 105.)

Exterior/**CYPRESS ALLEY**/Day

Through a gap in this alley of tall trees we see HUGH OATCAKE and the other picnickers race up the hillside. As they reach the gap, we PAN right and let the STEADICAM follow BEATRICE, HERO, and the Company as they run down the dip in the alley and up the other side towards the house. The STEADICAM chases them. Runs in front of them. Gives us their point of view.

Exterior/**VINEYARD**/Day

The horsemen in the distance. We RACK FOCUS to see FRANCIS SEACOLE running breathlessly towards us. As he flies past the camera, we PAN and TRACK left at great speed along parallel lines of vines stretching down the hill away from us. Up each of the alleys come roaring our increasingly fatigued picnickers. A panting and wheezing LEONATO brings up the rear.

Exterior/**DIRT ROAD**/Day

WIDE SHOT OF DON PEDRO'S men.

Exterior/**DON PEDRO'S POINT OF VIEW OF VILLA FROM THE ROAD**/Day

We see frantic activity in front of the villa. Farm workers scurry around, and on the highest roof we see a flag of welcome raised. CUT. CLOSE ON GEORGE SEACOLE raising flag. CLOSE on the flag.

Exterior/**DIRT ROAD**/Day

Wide shot reaction to the flag being raised. All six lead riders throw their arms in the air, as one. CUT to

Interior/**WOMEN'S BEDROOM**/Day

STEADICAM moving frantically in this large, uncluttered, cool, dormitory-style bedroom. Catching clothes as they fly through the air.

Slightly blurred coming into focus.

▶ Language Pointers ◀

- The **description** in a **screenplay** is the way in which the shots are described in clear, visual **images** for the director.
- Those **descriptions** will be largely dependent on the **locations**, or places, where each piece of action occurs.

PREPARING Continued

4. Add any new **technical terms** you have come across to your list. Jot down or draw (if appropriate), what you think they are. Write down three main differences between the **screenplay** and the original lines from the play.

   The writing of the **screenplay** has to be as good as a novel's. Write down two examples where the screenwriter's **descriptions** make it very clear what **mood** he wants to create.

5. Copy the film script layout sheet below. Choose your three favourite camera shots from the film script and then fill in all the necessary details. An example has been started for you.

Shot No.	Description	Picture/sketch	Camera position	Sound effects
Example	flags coming over hill		long-shot	hooves drumming
1				
2				
3				

PRESENTING

6. One of the problems you may have had when drawing the shots was the amount of movement. That's why it's better, certainly to start with, to write, rather than draw the film, although you must think visually.

   Your turn:
   - In pairs, write the opening of a film script called 'The Party'.
   - Use four different **locations** and a variety of camera positions/movements to create an atmosphere of anticipation.
   - Limit the amount of **dialogue** to a bare minimum.

FOLLOW-UP

7. List as many **verbs** of speed and movement from Kenneth Brannagh's **screenplay** as you can.

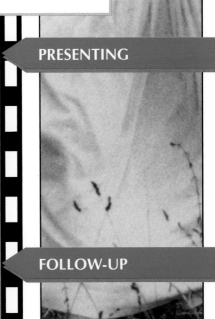

- Identify differences between an original pre-twentieth century text and a modern screenplay.
- Write an essay comparing screenplay with other forms of writing.

Classic lines

STARTING

1. It has been the fashion for some years now to take established classics of literature and turn them into TV series or films. However, on first impression some of these texts look less than promising. Read the opening of *Sense and Sensibility* by Jane Austen.

The family of Dashwood had been long settled in Sussex. Their estate was large, and their residence was at Norland Park, in the centre of their property, where, for many generations, they had lived in so respectable a manner, as to engage the general good opinion of their surrounding acquaintance. The late owner of this estate was a single man, who lived to a very advanced age, and who for many years of his life, had a constant companion and housekeeper in his sister. But her death, which happened ten years before his own, produced a great alteration in his home; for to supply her loss, he invited and received into his house the family of his nephew Mr Henry Dashwood, the legal inheritor of the Norland estate, and the person to whom he intended to bequeath it. In the society of his nephew and niece, and their children, the old Gentleman's days were comfortably spent. His attachment to them all increased. The constant attention of Mr and Mrs Henry Dashwood to his wishes, which proceeded not merely from interest, but from goodness of heart, gave him every degree of solid comfort which his old age could receive; and the cheerfulness of the children added a relish to his existence.

By a former marriage, Mr Henry Dashwood had one son: by his present lady, three daughters. The son, a steady respectable young man, was amply provided for by the fortune of his mother, which had been large, and half of which devolved on him on his coming of age. By his own marriage, likewise, which happened soon afterwards, he added to his wealth. To him therefore the succession of the Norland estate was not so really important as to his sisters; for their fortune, independent of what might arise to them from their father's inheriting that property, could be but small. Their mother had nothing, and their father only seven thousand pounds in his disposal; for the remaining moiety of his first wife's fortune was also secured to her child, and he had only a life interest in it.

2. Referring to the passage, copy and complete as much of the following table as you can.

Locations	Characters	Events
	old owner (no name) his sister (no name)	death of late owner's sister
		nephew and family move in
		old owner dies

3. Now read the opening of the **screenplay** in groups of four. One member of each group should read the stage directions.

Sense and Sensibility: The Screenplay

0 EXT. OPEN ROADS. NIGHT. TITLE SEQUENCE.
A series of travelling shots. A well-dressed, pompous-looking individual (JOHN DASHWOOD, 35) is making an urgent journey on horseback. He looks anxious.

1 EXT. NORLAND PARK. ENGLAND. MARCH 1800. NIGHT.
Silence. Norland Park, a large country house built in the early part of the eighteenth century, lies in the moonlit parkland.

2 INT. NORLAND PARK. MR DASHWOOD'S BEDROOM. NIGHT.
In the dim light shed by the candles we see a bed in which a MAN (MR DASHWOOD, 52) lies – his skin is waxy, his breathing laboured. Around him two silhouettes move and murmur, their clothing susurrating in the deathly hush. DOCTORS. A WOMAN (MRS DASHWOOD, 50) sits by his side, holding his hand, her eyes never leaving his face.

(Continued on page 110.)

Classic lines

(Continued from
page 109.)

MR DASHWOOD (*urgent*)
Is John not yet arrived?
MRS DASHWOOD
We expect him at any moment, dearest.
MR DASHWOOD *looks anguished.*
The girls – I have left so little.
MRS DASHWOOD
Shh, hush, Henry.
MR DASHWOOD
Elinor will try to look after you all, but make sure she finds a
good husband. The men are such noodles hereabouts, little
wonder none has pleased her.

They smile at each other. MRS DASHWOOD *is just managing to conceal
her fear and grief.*

MRS DASHWOOD
But Marianne is sure to find her storybook hero.
MR DASHWOOD
A romantic poet with flashing eyes and empty pockets?
MRS DASHWOOD
As long as she loves him, who*ever* he is.
MR DASHWOOD
Margaret will go to sea and become a pirate so we need not
concern ourselves with her.

MRS DASHWOOD *tries to laugh but it emerges as a sob. An older*
MANSERVANT (THOMAS) *now enters, anxiety written on every
feature.*

THOMAS
Your son is arrived from London, sir.

MR DASHWOOD *squeezes his wife's hand.*

MR DASHWOOD
Let me speak to John alone.

She nods quickly and he smiles at her with infinite tenderness.

MR DASHWOOD
Ah, my dear. How happy you have made me.

▶ **Language Pointer** ◀

● The **pace** of a piece of writing can be dependent on a number of things. In a film, the sudden entrance or exit of a character, or quick cutting from one scene or shot to another, can create a sense of speed or fast **pace**.

MRS DASHWOOD *makes a superhuman effort and smiles back. She allows* THOMAS *to help her out. She passes* JOHN DASHWOOD *as he enters, presses his hand, but cannot speak.* JOHN *takes her place by the bed.*

JOHN

Father …

MR DASHWOOD *summons his last ounce of energy and starts to whisper with desperate intensity.*

4. Now copy and complete a table identical to the one you did earlier, but this time for the **screenplay**.

PREPARING 2

Locations	Characters	Events
open roads	John Dashwood	riding back

In pairs, discuss the differences between the two tables.
Look at:

● the number of **locations** and the way in which they are described
● the difference in **pace** between the two
● the way in which **characters** are introduced.

5. Write a substantial essay detailing everything you have learned so far about **screenplays**. Your essay should be well structured and should focus on how **screenplays** are different from other forms of writing. Use concrete examples from the three scripts you have looked at.

PRESENTING

The three elements of your essay should be:

● the way the text appears on the page – how it's set out/layout
● the choice of language (**tenses**, sentence **structure**, etc.)
● what you feel the key skills of good **screenplay** writing are.

FOCUS FOCUS

- Research and write a treatment and sample scenes for a film screenplay.
- Role-play a meeting between producer and director to discuss a treatment.
- Write an evaluation of the treatment.

The business

STARTING

1. This book is all about developing language skills in real writing situations, whether it be in a **commercial** setting, or a personal one. The final unit looks at taking creative writing skills and applying them to a **commercial** setting.

People who want to get a **screenplay** made into a film go about it in a number of ways. They might:

- write a whole **screenplay** and then try to find a producer
- write a **treatment** (a summary of the story) plus some sample scenes and find a producer
- write nothing except the **treatment** and find a producer.

You are a young writer who wants to break into film. You are aware that in recent years there has been a lot of success for adaptations of classic stories, either real-life drama from history or from famous novels, particularly British ones. You are also aware that there is a producer who is willing to put money into the making of another one. However, you need to do *two* things, even to be considered:

- produce a written **treatment**
- have a personal meeting with the producer at which you **pitch** your idea.

▶ **Language Pointers** ◀

- A **treatment** is an early outline of a film that provides a summary of the key scenes, **characters**, the main action, who the likely **audience** are, and perhaps reference to costs and lengths of time needed to make the film.
- The **treatment** is often presented when you **pitch** – or sell the idea – to a producer, director or a film company.

PREPARING

2. The story you have settled on is the real-life drama of Lord Nelson, and in particular the Battle of Trafalgar. You have done some **research** on the historical background and come up with the following information. Read it through carefully.

Biographical Notes

1758–1805
Horatio Nelson
b. Burnham Thorpe, Norfolk

1770:	Joined Navy
1784:	Sent to West Indies (married Frances Nisbet there)
1793–1794:	At war with France, lost sight in right eye when commanding naval brigade at Bastia
1796:	Santa Cruz: lost his right arm
1798:	Destroyed Napoleon's fleet in Egypt. Returned to Naples, began love-affair with Emma, Lady Hamilton
1801:	Made rear-admiral, led attack on Copenhagen
1805:	Greatest victory against combined French/Spanish at Trafalgar (off coast of south-west Spain) but mortally wounded on flagship *HMS Victory*

There is more source material overleaf.

The business

Your **research** has also led you to look at the following letter written by Nelson to Lady Hamilton on the eve of the Battle of Trafalgar. Their relationship is one possible **focus** for your film, so you need to read it carefully.

> Victory Oct 19: 1805
> Noon Cadiz E/E 16 Leagues
>
> My Dearest beloved Emma the dear friend of my bosom the signal has been made that the Enemys combined fleet are coming out of Port. We have very little Wind so that I have no hopes of seeing them before tomorrow May the God of Battles crown my endeavours with success at all events I will take care that my name shall ever be most dear to you and Horatia both of whom I love as much as my own life, and as my last writing before the battle will be to you so I hope in God that I shall live to finish my career after the Battle. May Heaven bless you prays your Nelson Bronte.
>
> Oct 20th; in the morning we will close to the mouth of the Straights but the wind had not come far enough to the Westward to allow the combined fleets to weather the shoals off Trafalgar but they were counted as far as forty sail of ships of War which I suppose to be 34 of the line and six frigates, a Group of them was seen off the Lighthouse of Cadiz this morning but it blows so very fresh I think Westerly that I rather believe they will go into the Harbour before night. May God Almighty give us success over these fellows and enable us to get a Peace.

The letter was never finished. It was found open on Nelson's desk by Captain Hardy and taken to Lady Hamilton after the battle in which, of course, Nelson died.

Language Pointers

- The **focus** of a story, or main action, is the main plot which will drive the story.
- The **angle**, or slant, of the film is the view or attitude the writier or director wishes to convey. For example, the director or writer may wish to portray Nelson as a traditional hero.

Further **research** into the letter reveals the following new details:

- 'Horatia' is the name of Nelson and Emma Hamilton's little daughter.
- 'Nelson Bronte' is the rest of his name, although his first name 'Horatio' is more commonly known.
- Nelson died in HMS Victory's cockpit in the arms of his friend Captain Hardy, having been shot by a French sharpshooter.

On your own, make some notes about what the letter reveals about Nelson's character. Consider:

- whether he comes across as a family man
- how fond he is of Lady Hamilton
- what most of the letter is about.

It is time for you to decide the **focus** of your film and **screenplay** and how it will be shown (what will actually happen in the film).

PLANNING

There are a number of possibilities:

- The love affair between Nelson and Emma Hamilton.
- The heroic qualities of Nelson.
- Nelson, the adulterer, who betrays his wife.
- Nelson's life from birth to death.
- Any other possibility you choose.

When you have considered these, note down your decision, and also what **angle** you are going to take. In other words, what view will you give of Nelson: a man obsessed by winning; a loving, family man or perhaps a man to be despised because he left his wife?

You are now in a position to begin drawing out the first few scenes, or shots, from the film.

SCRIPT & SPEECH 3

The business

3. Sketch out your first three or four shots of the film, and add **captions** to go with them. Here are examples of two possible opening sequences:

The French are defeated in Egypt.

Nelson being introduced to Lady Hamilton.

4. Now look at this sample **'visualisation'** of the opening shots:

e.g. Egypt. A man stands with his back to us on the deck of a ship, smoke swirling around him. Men dash about, tying ropes, firing cannons. In the background, the smoke clears and we see the prow of a French ship disappearing into the water. The man turns and walks towards the camera – it is Nelson.

▶ **Language Pointers** ◀

● A **treatment** is a full explanation of a film's story, possibly including lively camera angles, key scenes or sets etc.
● A **pitch** is an attempt by someone, usually a writer, to sell an idea for a story to a producer or director.

PLANNING Continued

5. Look carefully at the example and then decide:

● which **tense** is used
● how the camera's view is given
● which details are needed to 'paint' the scene clearly.

Now write your own **visualisation** of the opening scenes.

6. Next you need to write something that will sell the film.

The treatment

Normally you'd write a full-length **treatment** telling the main story of the film. For now, you are simply going to compose a **one-line pitch**. That is to say, write a sentence or two in which you sum up the proposed film.

Here are two examples; one is from a real film, the second is made up.

A quiet American beach. Blue water. Peace. Suddenly, a monstrous beast shatters the silence, and rips apart Amityville. A beast by the name of 'Jaws' – a man-eating shark.

A love affair that spans the centuries. An English city. Two children, one rich, one poor, flung together because of one act of kindness, split apart because of one act of treachery. Will they ever be together? In their story, *Romeo and Juliet* meets *Coronation Street* and *Titanic* meets *Gone With the Wind*.

The business

7. Write your **one-line** (approximately) **pitch**. Now, in pairs, **role-play** the meeting between producer and writer. You must each have a go at both **roles**.

The writer's job

- Sum up the film vividly and with enthusiasm (use your written **pitch** if you want).
- Verbally, sketch out the main story – where the film begins, how it ends, etc.
- Say why it MUST be made – why people will go to see it.
- Say who would play the leading parts (real actors).

The producer's job

- Question the likely interest in the film.
- Be worried about the cost.
- Question aspects of the story you don't like (e.g. if the writer wants to focus on the love affair, say you're more interested in the battles).
- Say you'd like to change certain aspects – the ending? (Nelson doesn't die!)
- Decide whether you're interested in making the film or not (based on how persuasive the writer is).

---

8. Write a full **evaluation** of how successful the **pitch** was. Did you persuade the producer?

Write the opening sequences for the film in the form of a proper **screenplay**. Check back over previous units to revise **screenplay** layout and language techniques.

Assessment

- *Complete a range of reading and writing assessments.*
- *Revisit some of the skills you have already learned.*
- *Work to deadlines in an exam situation.*

This unit includes a variety of tests that will enable you to see how you cope working on your own and with timed tasks. The tests do not, however, cover everything you have done, and your class and homework assignments are equally important.

Your teacher will decide

- how long you have on each task
- whether you can use dictionaries or other forms of reference
- whether you can refer to the relevant sections in the book
- whether you can ask for help or advice
- how many marks are available for each question
- your teacher has a mark scheme available.

The assessment is divided into **two papers**: a test of reading and a test of writing skills. There is work at **WORD, SENTENCE** and **WHOLE TEXT** level. That's to say there is work on individual words (what they mean, how they are used), work on sentences (sentence grammar and word order), and work on understanding and responding to whole texts (what they mean and how they are put together).

REMEMBER

- Read the questions carefully.
- Write clearly and neatly.
- Check for accuracy in spelling, punctuation and grammar.
- Time yourself carefully – if the assessment is timed.

Paper 1: reading

The following extract is taken from a letter written on behalf of Chief Seattle, leader of the Dwamish, Suqamish and other allied Indian tribes, to the President of the United States, Franklin Pierce, in 1854. The US government was trying to persuade the Chief to sell his lands and hand them over to US rule. Read it carefully and complete the tasks that follow.

Letter from Chief Seattle

How can you buy or sell the sky, the warmth of the land? The idea is strange to us.

If we do not own the freshness of the air and the sparkle of the water, how can you buy them?

Every part of this earth is sacred to my people.

Every shining pine needle, every sandy shore, every mist in the dark woods, every clearing and humming insect is holy in the memory and experience of my people. The sap which courses through the trees carried the memories of the red man.

The white man's dead forget the country of their birth when they go to walk among the stars. Our dead never forget this beautiful earth, for it is the mother of the red man.

We are part of the earth and it is part of us. The perfumed flowers are our sisters; the deer, the horse, the great eagle, these are our brothers.

The rocky crests, the juices in the meadows, the body heat of the pony, and man – all belong to the same family.

So, when the Great Chief in Washington sends word that he wishes to buy our land, he asks much of us. The Great Chief sends word he will reserve us a place so that we can live comfortably to ourselves.

He will be our father and we will be his children. So we will consider your offer to buy our land.

But it will not be easy. For this land is sacred to us.

This shining water that moves in the streams and rivers is not just water but the blood of our ancestors.

If we sell you land, you must remember that it is sacred, and you must teach your children that it is sacred and that each ghostly reflection in the clear water of the lakes tells of events and memories in the life of my people.

The water's murmur is the voice of my father's father.

The rivers are our brothers, they quench our thirst. The rivers carry our canoes, and feed our children. If we sell you our land, you must remember, and teach your children, that the rivers are our brothers, and yours, and you must henceforth give the rivers the kindness you would give any brother.

We know that the white man does not understand our ways. One portion of land is the same to him as the next, for he is a stranger who comes in the night and takes from the land whatever he needs.

The earth is not his brother, but his enemy, and when he has conquered it, he moves on.

He leaves his father's graves behind, and he does not care. He kidnaps the earth from his children, and he does not care.

His father's grave and his children's birthright, are forgotten. He treats his mother, the earth, and his brother, the sky, as things to be bought, plundered, sold like sheep or bright beads.

His appetite will devour the earth and leave behind only a desert.

I do not know. Our ways are different from your ways.

The sight of your cities pains the eyes of the red man. But perhaps it is because the red man is a savage and does not understand.

There is no quiet place in the white man's cities. No place to hear the unfurling of leaves in spring, or the rustle of an insect's wings.

But perhaps it is because I am a savage and do not understand.

The clatter only seems to insult the ears. And what is there to life if a man cannot hear the lonely cry of the whippoorwill or the arguments of the frogs around a pond at night? I am a red man and do not understand.

TASK ONE	The first two questions that start the passage contain at least seven nouns – each referring to nature. List them.

TASK TWO	These first two questions are both rhetorical questions. Explain what this means. It may help you to think how they are different from a question such as 'What time will you be coming back from the party?'

TASK THREE	The passage uses two tenses – the present and the future – more than any others. Copy the table and tick the appropriate box.

	present	future
a. Every part of this earth is sacred		
b. We will consider your offer		
c. The rivers are our brothers		
d. His appetite will devour the earth		

TASK FOUR	The passage is full of descriptions of the natural world using the structure of premodifying adjectives, e.g. *sandy shore* in which the adjective (*sandy*) comes *before* the noun (*shore*). List *six* other examples of premodifying adjectives relating to nature in the passage.

TASK FIVE	In your own words, write down *three* things that Chief Seattle criticises about the 'white man's' way of life in the passage.

| **TASK SIX** | Explain, with close reference to the text, how Chief Seattle makes the reader sympathetic to the views he is expressing. Your answer should be thorough and you should comment on:

a. the use of rhetorical questions
b. the use of repetition
c. the use of antithesis (when two ideas are contrasted)
d. the description of the red man's life
e. particularly powerful words, phrases or sentences. |
|---|---|

Paper 2: writing

TASK ONE

The following words, phrases and sentences are all taken from another section of the letter sent by Chief Seattle. The sequence has been mixed up. Write it down in the most likely order. Punctuation and capitals will need to be added. The line at the top is the real first line.

- I have seen a thousand rotting buffaloes on the prairie
- how the smoking iron horse
- for whatever happens to the beasts, soon happens to man
- left by the white man who shot them
- can be more important than the buffalo that we kill
- from a passing train
- man would die from a great loneliness of spirit
- I am a savage and do not understand
- only to stay alive
- what is man without the beasts
- if all the beasts were gone

TASK TWO (EXTENDED WRITING)

Extended writing: choose any **TWO** of the following assignments:

a. Write a letter in reply to Chief Seattle from the office of the President. Keeping in mind that the letter was written in 1854, give your reasons why it is important to allow the white man to develop the land, allow railways to be built and so on. The vocabulary should be equally vivid and create clear images of the advantages of development and industrialisation.

b. Write an ode (poem of praise) of at least twelve lines praising the way of life of the Native American Indian and regretting its disappearance. It should provide a similar picture to that given by Chief Seattle and should feature the use of premodifying adjectives and nouns (*the sandy shore*).

c. A local pond in a small wood where you played as a child, caught tiddlers, met with friends, and where other children in years gone by also played, is to be destroyed and replaced with a car park for local businesses. You have the chance to speak at a town planners' meeting. Write the speech you will give. Make sure you use as many of the following speech-making skills as you can:

- Opposing pairs.
- Repetition.
- Emotional appeal.
- Rhetorical questions.
- Patterns of three (ideas).
- Strong images.

Mark predictions

When you have finished the assessment, copy out the table below and keep it as a record to refer to later.

Marks available	Your prediction	Actual mark
Paper 1		
TASK 1		
TASK 2		
TASK 3		
TASK 4		
TASK 5		
TASK 6		
Paper 2		
TASK 1		
TASK 2 a		
b		
c		
Total marks available	**Predicted total**	**Actual total**

Final level/grade

Glossary

accent 97 The way words are spoken/pronounced, usually associated with a particular region, e.g. saying *'ole'* instead of *'hole'*.

adjective 7, 45 An **adjective** describes a **noun** and is often in front of it – the *quick, brown* fox. It is also used with the **verb** 'to be' – he is *foolish* and *unreliable*.

adverb 7, 43 An **adverb** modifies a sentence, and explains how a **verb** works – she slid *dangerously*. It can control an **adjective** or another **adverb** – it was *so* ugly or he played *really badly*.

alliteration 69, 77 The use of two or more words that begin with the same sound to create an interesting effect, e.g. *foul, fog* of *fumes*.

angle 115, 117 In film-making, this is the view or attitude the writer or director wishes to convey, e.g. *Mrs Dashwood is a fussy woman.*

annotate 63, 67, 75, 84, 99 If you **annotate** a piece of writing, you write over it, underline words or phrases, make notes around it, and so on.

antithesis 88–89 The positioning of opposite ideas to create a specific effect. The use of **antithesis** is a **speech technique**, that is, a device for making speech effective.

archaic (form/verbs) 43 The use of antiquated words that are no longer in everyday use, but may be used on formal occasions.

argument 63–66 The term **argument** can be applied to a text to mean the view that is being conveyed by the writer. It does not mean 'argument' in the sense of conflict, necessarily.

audience 9, 50, 55, 62, 64–65, 81, 113 The people addressed by the text; in a book this would be the reader.

autobiography 16, 21, 23 This comes from Greek and means, literally, 'self, life, write'. An **autobiography** is usually written in the first person.

biographer 31 Someone who writes a **biography**.

biography 16, 21, 23, 31 An account of someone's life written by another person. A **biography** is usually written in the third person.

black comedy 36–37 Humour with a darker or more serious side, perhaps finding laughter in death or unhappiness.

caption 116 This is a word or sentence that goes with a picture to explain what it shows. The **caption** is usually placed underneath.

character 37–38, 65, 82, 111, 113 An individual in a play or story. The actions and **dialogue** of a **character** can be used by the author to infer the individual's personality.

cliché 95 A phrase or opinion that has become overused and lacks originality, e.g. *I was so scared, I felt a shiver down my spine.*

colloquialism 53 This is usually taken to mean an informal phrase or expression that is used in a particular country or place, and can be difficult to understand for non-native speakers (e.g. *'fluffed it'*).

comedy see **black comedy**.

commercial 112 Related to the buying and selling of merchandise.

computer game (program, hero, quest, narrative, location, characters, objects, territory, rooms, world) 34–38. A **computer game** or **program** may contain a **hero** with a **quest** which drives the **narrative**. The **hero** moves around and encounters a number of **characters** and **objects** in a central area or **territory** (e.g. castle, planet or town). The **location** is one of a range of places that can be visited within a particular **territory** (e.g. in *Discworld* there are **rooms**). All these devices help to establish the **world** of the game.

conceit 8–9 A **conceit** is an extravagant comparison. It is often a clever fantasy or set of language tricks linked to one idea, conjured up to amuse and entertain an **audience**.

CV 52–53 **Curriculum Vitae.** A brief description of the education, qualifications, employment details, skills and interests of an individual.

description 100–101, 103, 107 In a **screenplay** this is the way in which the shots are described in clear, visual **images** for the director.

dialogue 35, 37–38, 107 Another word for conversation.

discourse 65 A conversation, or a formal and informative talk or item of text on a particular topic.

draft 102 The first attempt at a written document; the same document may go through many **drafts** before reaching its final **draft** stage.

ellipsis 41 The omission from a sentence of words that are not needed to complete the sense of a sentence. An author may, for example, miss out some of the words to shorten a quotation without losing the sense; this will be marked with three dots ...

euphemism 67 You use **euphemisms** when you wish to disguise, or soften the impact of the truth, e.g. *I need to spend a penny*, instead of *I need the toilet*.

evaluation 118 Assessing the state of something.

exaggerate 9–11 To give an impression of something as being bigger or greater than it actually is. It can be associated with **satire**.

exterior 103, 105 In this case, a **technical term** to mean an outside **location**.

features editor 77 A job on a magazine involving overseeing any special topics or articles about a specific thing, e.g. fashion or sport.

fiction see **narrative fiction**.

focus 114–115, 117 The **focus** of a story is the main idea that will drive the story.

form 36, 72, 75 In this case, the way in which text is presented or arranged, including its **structure**.

formal speech (language) see **speech**.

genre 36, 38, 54, 69 A **genre** is a type of writing with specific characteristics. There are many different **genres** of writing, e.g. comic, **narrative**, adventure.

heroic quatrain see **quatrain.**

iambic pentameter 64–65 A line of **verse**, usually of ten syllables, that contains five 'stresses', each generally falling on the second syllable of each word.

image (imagery) 71–73, 75, 78, 84, 89, 91, 93–94, 100–101, 107 The creation of word pictures in a reader's mind.

implied meanings 29 The way in which something is suggested, rather than simply explained, in the text. This is often achieved through the use of **symbol** or **metaphor**.

in memoriam 77 In memory of (a dead person, usually).

inanimate 59 Something without life, such as an object.

inaugural speech see **speech**.

interior 103 In this case a **technical term** to mean an inside **location**.

interpret 98–99 In this case, to perform the **role** of a character in a certain way.

inter-textuality 68–69 The deliberate mixing of different types of **genre** or text to create a specific effect.

juxtaposition 101, 103 The placing together of two things – ideas, words, **images** and so on, for a particular effect.

language, (formal) see **speech**

linguistic 102 Related to the way **language** works.

location 37–38, 105, 107, 109, 111 A place or setting for a film. See also **computer game**.

lyrics (lyric poetry) 74–76, 78 Commonly understood as meaning *'the words of pop songs'*. **Lyric poetry** is the name given to a particular **style** of **verse** that presents a poet's feelings in a simple, direct way.

metaphor 29, 75, 91, 94–95 A direct comparison of two, normally unrelated ideas. A **metaphor** compares two things by saying that something is something else, e.g. *a blanket of clouds*.

mock-heroic 33, 36, 38 The term for writing which constantly sets itself up as grand and then immediately, humorously, undercuts that effect with the ordinariness of what follows.

modal form (verb) 41 The **mood** of a **verb** is suggested by its **modal form**.

mood 41, 44–46, 71, 100, 107 The general atmosphere of a piece of writing, similar to **tone**.

narrative (fiction) 11, 16, 21, 23, 36–37 Relating to any linked chain of events told by someone – usually a story. **Narrative fiction** is an idea or piece of text that has been invented by the writer or speaker. Sometimes a piece of **fiction** may have an element of **truth** in it, e.g. an author might write about the **fictional** childhood of a little boy, but may **locate** the story in a real town.

noun 7 A **noun** is a naming word.

ode 58–61, 78 A poem written in praise of an object or person, usually **rhymed**.

one-line pitch see **pitch**.

pace 71, 97, 99, 111 The speed or rate at which a piece of writing progresses when read.

paragraph (indented, blocked) 9, 19 Begins a new line, usually with a new topic, change of time or place and is either **indented** (set in from the margin) or **blocked** (arranged with a whole line space between each **paragraph**).

personification 59 If you use **personification** in writing, you give human characteristics to something **inanimate** – such as an object.

persuasive language (argument) 64, 68–69 The use of particular words or phrases to convey strong opinions or **viewpoints**.

pitch (one-line) 97, 112–113, 117–118 An attempt by someone, usually a writer, to sell an idea for a story to a producer or director. A **one-line pitch** is a sentence or two to sum up the **proposal** of a film.

pronoun (subject, object, possessive) 23, 43 A **pronoun** is used instead of, or to indicate, a **noun** already mentioned or known. A **subject pronoun** uses the subject of the sentence; an **object pronoun** uses the object; a **possessive pronoun** uses the **possessive**.

proposal 38 A plan or suggestion.

quatrain (heroic quatrain) 62–65 A four-line part, or **stanza**, of a poem. A **heroic quatrain** rhymes *abab*.

quest 36–38 A challenge that the **hero** of a story is given.

refrain 67 A line or phrase that a writer comes back to again and again, like a familar melody in a piece of music.

religious echoes 87 In this context, the **audience** responds to the religious **style** of the speaker with the words '*Amen*'.

repetition 46, 51, 67, 75, 83 The **noun** form of the verb 'to repeat'.

research 113–115 To gather background information on a particular subject, often in order to form conclusions about that subject.

resolution 75 An ending that resolves or sums up key points.

rhetorical question 84–85 A **rhetorical question** is one that expects only one answer and is used as a **persuasive** device, e.g. '*We don't have to accept this do we?*'

rhyme (couplet) 47, 58–59, 62–63, 65–66, 69, 72–73, 75, 77, 97 The similarity of sound between words or endings of words, e.g. *big, wig*. A **rhyming couplet** is two lines of adjacent **verse**, usually of the same length.

rhythm 75, 97, 99 The beat or regular pattern of a poem or song.

role (role-play) 65, 98, 118 The **character** someone plays. This may be in a film or play or it might be as an exercise, e.g. two students might **role-play** a discussion between a parent and teacher.

satire (satirical) 10–11, 36–37 A form of writing that seeks to make fun of something, someone, or set of ideas in a sharp and sometimes cruel way.

setting 102–103 In this case, the situation in which a film is set, e.g. the time, place, scenery, etc.

screenplay (description, location) 100, 103, 105, 107, 109, 111–112, 115, 118 The script for a film. A **screenplay description** is the way in which the shots are described in clear, visual **images** for the director. **Screenplay locations** are where each piece of action occurs.

simile 57, 75, 91 A phrase that compares two things, containing 'as' or 'like', e.g. *her hair was as bright as gold.*

simple language 27 Sometimes used to convey meaning without key parts of a clause such as a **verb,** e.g. a message saying '*In danger*'.

sonnet 62–66 A poem of fourteen lines that generally follows a regular **rhyme** pattern and ends with a couplet.

speech (formal, natural, inaugural, technique) 53, 80–81, 83–87, 89, 97, 99 A **formal speech** is prepared, and normally uses **standard English** vocabulary and grammar. **Natural speech** is **speech** that is unprepared and may contain informal language and expressions. An **inaugural speech** is one given at the official ceremony when a president or other newly appointed leader or officer takes office. A **speech technique** is a device for making a **speech** effective.

standard English 25 The accepted form of English as it would be written in business correspondence and other formal texts.

stanza 63 A set of lines or **verse** in poetry, the pattern of which is generally repeated throughout the poem.

structure 35, 43, 47, 51, 63–64, 111 The way a piece of writing, e.g. a poem, is organised and set out.

style 15, 75, 85, 87–88, 91, 103 A manner of writing, e.g. dramatic, comic, **satirical**.

symbol (symbolic) 29, 71–73 A **symbol** is an object or **image** used to represent or carry strong meanings (e.g. an apple to denote youth, freshness, health).

technical terms (language) 68–69, 105, 107 In film-making, these are the words and phrases usually connected with the actual process of shooting the film.

technique see **speech technique.**

tense (present, present simple, present continuous, past, future, conditional) 41, 43, 51, 111, 117 **Tense** is the form a **verb** takes to indicate the time that the action takes place. The **present tense** is used when the action is currently happening, e.g. *I dance.* The **present simple** is often considered useful in terms of style in poetry, avoiding the repetition of 'ing', i.e. the **present continuous** *I dance*, rather than *I am dancing.* The **past tense** is used when the action has already occurred, e.g. *I danced.* The **future tense** is used when the action will happen in the future, e.g. *I will dance.* The **conditional** form *would* can be used with the *if* clause, e.g. *If I had more money, I'd travel around the world.*

tone (intimate) 36, 38, 44–47, 56–57, 71 The manner of expression in a piece of writing. An **intimate tone** is where the relationship between the reader and writer is very close.

transcript 25 A record of **speech**, written exactly as spoken, word for word.

treatment 112–113, 117 An early outline of a film that provides a summary of the key scenes, **characters**, the main action, details of the likely **audience**, and potential costs.

triolet 73 A poem of eight lines with two **rhymes** that reoccur throughout the poem.

truth see **narrative fiction.**

verb 7, 23, 27, 41, 48, 50–51, 107 A **verb** describes an action or a state – she *hurried* down the hall, she *wondered* who it could be.

verse 43, 47, 54–55, 65, 75, 94 A single, complete section of a poem, or song, sometimes taken to mean 'poetry' in general.

viewpoint 51, 64 Expressing a particular opinion about something, see also **persuasive argument**.

visualisation 116 To describe something as if you were seeing it.

vocabulary 82–83, 97 The range of possible words available to a speaker or writer.